Bright Advent

Bright Advent

Robert Strong

Marie Alexander Poetry Series, Volume 21

Robert Alexander, Series Editor
Nickole Brown, Editor

WHITE PINE PRESS / BUFFALO, NEW YORK

White Pine Press
PO Box 236
Buffalo, NY 14201
www.whitepine.org

Acknowledgments:
Early selections from this book appeared in *Hotel Amerika* (TransGenre Issue), Vol. 7, No. 2; *Common-place.org* (Poetic Research section), Vol. 10, No. 4; *Rethinking History,* Vol. 15, No. 1; and *Modern Language Studies Journal,* Vol. 45, No. 1.

Deep gratitude to Nickole Brown and Robert Alexander at the Marie Alexander Series, as well as Dennis Maloney and Elaine LaMattina at White Pine Press, for making this book. I owe many thanks to the keen readers and thinkers who contributed to the shaping of this project: Danielle Dutton, Karla Kelsey, Richard Greenfield, Elizabeth Bradfield, Meredith Neuman, Catherine E. Kelly, and Christine DeLucia, as well as Paul Erickson, Jim Moran, and every librarian, editor, and archivist at both the American Antiquarian Society and *Common-place*. And always: Hillory.

Research for this project was completed with the generous support of a Fellowship for Creative and Performing Artists and Writers at the American Antiquarian Society.

Publication of this book was made possible, in part, by public funds from the New York State Council on the Arts with the support of Governor Andrew M. Cuomo and the New York State Legislature, a State Agency, and with the support of Robert Alexander.

Cover by Jennika Smith.

Printed and bound in the United States of America.

ISBN 978-1-945680-04-5

Library of Congress number 2016949219

Contents

Bright Advent

HISTORIAN'S INTRODUCTION

Bright Advent invites us into the seventeenth-century Northeast, a region of pine trees and cornfields, whales and quahogs, iced-over inland ponds and heaving saltwater tides. Indigenous Algonquians conceived of this place as the Dawnland, where light first meets the continent each day, and where generations upon generations of ancestors had shaped, inhabited, and derived meaning from land, water, and other-than-human beings. In this deeply known and remembered place they intended to remain. Freshly arrived English colonists understood it as New England, where they struggled to transplant Old World ways into an often forbidding "wilderness," and to launch a project of societal purification in anticipation of the Second Coming of Christ. In this resource-rich place they intended to construct houses and fences, pasture livestock, and expand into the interior. Some colonists, notably the missionary John Eliot, also desired to bring puritan faith to the "heathens." But the indigenous residents of the Dawnland—Wampanoags, banakis, and many tribal relations—already possessed complex ways of being spiritual people, and of understanding their responsibilities to past, present, and future.

As these indigenous and colonial worlds grew increasingly entangled in the mid-1600s, tension, distrust, and outright resistance emerged. Violent crises broke out, like the Pequot War of the 1630s and King Philip's War of the 1670s, the latter of which brought pervasive, region-wide transformations to tribal and settler relations. *Bright Advent* journeys through a constellation of contested sites that shaped Native-settler encounters during these tumultuous times. It visits the "praying town" of Natick, where indigenous "converts" confronted multiple faith traditions; the printing press room where *Up-Biblum* God, a Native-language translation of Scripture, painstakingly assumed physical form; Assawampsett Pond, where the Native translator John Sassamon perished under questionable circumstances; and the animate, liminal shoreline that connected terrestrial areas to the Atlantic. While King Philip's War is the framing conflict, the poetry's focus is on the lead-up to it, and the intensely human, interior dimensions of those who endeavored to navigate and make meaning from worlds in flux.

In describing the translated Bible, Robert Strong invokes "the tension in binding these pages." This is an apt way to characterize the project of *Bright Advent*, and any attempt to make literary sense of an exceedingly contentious era, replete with strikingly diverse world-views and conceptions of time, space, signification. *Bright Advent* probes at borders, beginnings, and endings. Where and when does King Philip's War commence? Arguably not with Sassamon's frigid death in 1675, but in the multitude of minor and major tensions that accreted over a longer sweep of time. Where does creative license seep into the historical archive? Given that there has never been a singular, stable documentary archive—written sources have been unevenly preserved, published, lost, destroyed by fire and flood, kept secret from public view—we are urged to question its parameters, and to explore the signs that may lie beyond its inky, papery edges. The book's creative juxtaposition of archival and imaginative elements, plus the subtle device of single quotation marks delineating the two, is a provocation to re-examine the very nature of authority in storytelling about the past.

By assuming the form of poetry for this re-engagement with the seventeenth century, Strong joins a conversation with a host of earlier poets who have plumbed aspects of the war, including Robert Lowell, Susan Howe, and Louise Erdrich, as well as local and tribal writers across the Northeast. We might consider *Bright Advent* an inflection point, or a deep-dive into selected pools of significance, rather than any attempt to offer a final word on this era or a comprehensive accounting of all perspectives. Indeed, contestations over meaning remain today as descendant communities continue to grapple with the fallout of momentous violence and asymmetrical exercises of power. Strong writes in his afterword about "The project of colonialism. / The project of survival." These were the challenges of the 1600s, and they certainly remain so today—especially for the Dawnland peoples who endure, in places thickly layered with memories of pain and also regeneration.

—Christine DeLucia
Author of *The Memory Lands: King Philip's War and the Place of Violence in the Northeast*, Yale University Press.

SETTING AND CHARACTERS

The Bright Advent: In the 1600s, many Puritan colonists in Massachusetts Bay believed they labored during the Bright Advent, a period immediately prior to Christ's corporeal return to earth, when "the brightness of his coming" was bringing a terrific surge of supernatural power and human effort to revolutionize the course of world events. Thinking the Native Americans to be descendants of the lost tribes of Israel—who are prophesied to be converted to Christianity before Christ's second coming—some Puritans set about to hasten the Apocalypse by translating the entire Bible into Algonquian, training native preachers, and establishing "Praying Indian" towns.

Reverend John Eliot (1604-1690): Known as the Apostle to the Indians, Eliot was the chief colonial strategist for the missionary effort in Massachusetts Bay. He helped found thirteen "Praying Indian" towns and printed the so-called Indian Bible, the first published in the colonies in any language. The conversion of the Indians became his life's work.

John Sassamon (c. 1620-1675): A gifted, orphaned Massachusett Indian and translator for Eliot. He served as an interpreter and soldier for the Puritan colonists in the Pequot War, attended Harvard, translated the entire Bible into Algonquian with Eliot, and became a Christian minister. His murder, allegedly by agents of the Indian leader Metacom (Philip), precipitated King Philip's War.

Metacom (King Philip) (c. 1638-1676): Sachem of the Massachusett Pokanoket. The real roots of the war that bears Philip's name lay in the ongoing land grab by the English and the cultural and political pressures they inflicted on Native tribes. Additionally, Philip had reason to believe that his brother Alexander (Wamsutta), who died while in English custody, was poisoned. At the end of the war, Philip was shot dead, his wife and child were sold into slavery in the

Caribbean, and his head was stuck on a pike in Plymouth—the village where his father, Massasoit, had celebrated what some today call the "first Thanksgiving."

Grace Indian: An invented character. She belongs to Metacom's people.

Robert Boyle (1627-1691): One of the founders of modern chemistry, he is best known today for Boyle's Law of Gases. A wealthy and influential man who helped found The Royal Society, Boyle was also a devoted Christian who became president of the Corporation for the Propagation of the Gospel in New England, which funded Eliot's mission.

NOTE: all source material is from the seventeenth century and appears in single quotation marks.

Ask of me, and I shall give thee the heathen for thine inheritance, and the uttermost parts of the earth for thy possession.

Psalm 2:8

For then will I turn to the people a pure language, that they may all call upon the name of the Lord, to serve him with one consent.

Zephaniah 3:9

And then shall that Wicked be revealed, whom the Lord shall consume with the spirit of his mouth, and shall destroy with the brightness of his coming.

2 Thessalonians 2:8

Come over . . . and help us.

Acts 16:9; Massachusetts Bay Colony seal

THE MURDER, THE WAR

[John Sassamon found under the ice at Assawampsett Pond,
Nemasket (Middleborough), Massachusetts Bay Colony. January,
1675.]

caught between
what held him there
his mouth and throat
open to the cold box of air

> Indians said, He was fowling and fell
> at sunfall—an English fool
> for duck supper.

His head crowned up into ice spreading red—wine stained—
throat wine, mouth wine. His head, a chalice of hair, had to be
cut out with a dark halo of ice, lest further murder-like damage
occur before arriving at court.

> They said, Better to sleep hungry
> than go foolishly seeking,
> slip, and sink. Ice is also
> water.

opened out red
wet teeth frozen
on that second mouth open
in his throat
the tongue a muscle that goes
deep down enough
for two mouths

> They said, The throat did open
> from too much struggling upward
> against the ice.

in and out the water made
his lungs a tide—moon-moved air
moves in and out his mouth
open, slightly, to it.
The moon breathing him
three days (at most) caught
between the ice and the water

Assawampsett Pond affected by some network of wet pressures
the ocean ebb and flood up and down it went by mere inches
breathing in and out of his lungs for three days at most. Speaking
by way of whatever earth and moon did to that air. His halo hole
even freezing over for that most bitter cold and actual other ice
falling on all New England like vain temporary adornment.

the moon breathing his body three days
ice blind, throat open to the air
push and pull, flood and ebb

'He had been murthered, for his neck was broken by twisting of
his head round, which is the way the Indians some times use when
they practice murther; also, his head was extremely swollen, and
his body wounded in several parts of it. Taken out of the pond,
no water issued out of it, which argued that the Body was not
drowned, but dead before it came into the water.'

They said, 'Sometimes naughty Indians
would kill others' but never 'obscure as if
the dead Indian was not murthered.'

he came into the water
with dead air still
in the lungs

4

what air indicates is
it cannot be manipulated
if it be only contained
or
if it is only open sky (singular sky plural sky)
to the elements: pages blowing
its own pages: the mouth,
its press thus contained
cannot call anything anything

They said, Mattashunannamo, Tobias, and
       Tobias's son
are innocent of this death—present themselves
of their own free will here at court.

solid air in a box of water and ice
a more formal composition
three small axes could not break
but did obscure

at the first broadaxe crack it expiring
upward, the whole pond now breathes
out over the ice-lips and liquid gurgle
(throat of a whole pond saying,)
—*Oh*—
in neither explanation nor pain, only
some sudden obvious knowledge
gasps straight out and up

      dark birds scatter the snow

a rule of clear solid crowning
his head composed quite formally:

John Sassamon. In a cart to Plymouth, a three foot circle of red
    ice holding his head like a good cold thought.
A small squaw came for his body by way of hand gestures but
    English still need use of it.
Anyway, he is dead.
So be it. *Casus belli.*
This body is only the beginning.

~~~

When the Court ordered Tobias to approach the corpse, Sassamon's body began 'a bleeding afresh, as if it had been newly slain.'

> English said, May God have mercy on their souls
> and hanged the rascals. The son's rope breaking, he
> came then up from the ground in full pleading con-
> fession—an occasion for mercy, some said—had
> to be strung again with the rope red from his own
> dead father's neck.
> June 8, 1675

~~~

'If we pay them,   If they pay us
Paumogkut,   *Paumukqueog*

Not to pay them,   Not to pay us
Uppaumounnaout,   *Nuppaunukoounnanonut*

We pay not them,   They pay not us
Mat nuppaumounonog,   *Nuppaumukoounonog*

We did not pay them,   They did not pay us
Mat nuppaumounonuppaneg,   *Nuppaumukoounonuppanneg*

7

Let us pay them,   Let them pay us
   Paumontuh,   *Paumukqutteuh*

If we pay not them,   If they pay not us
Paumoogkut,   *Paumukooog'*

Pray
King Philip's men attack the town of Swansea, Sunday,
     June 24, 1675
9 dead English
June 26, The shadow of earth eclipses across the moon
Prey

'Thus did the War begin, this being the first English blood which
was spilt by the Indians in an hostile way. The Providence of God is
deeply observed, that the sword should be first drawn upon a day of
Humiliation, the Lord thereby declaring from heaven that he expects
something else from his People besides prayer and fasting.'

[And Before—1637, Pequot War]

Sassamon, a young man, 'in English clothes, and a gun in his hand.'

From a distance, a group of warring Pequots calls out: 'What are you? An Indian or an Englishman?'

'Come hither,' Sassamon shouted in their tongue, 'and I will tell you.'

When the Pequots came within range, the young interpreter 'pulls up his cock and let fly at one of them, and without question was the death of him.'

[And Before]

Sassamon encounters a dead man laid out by the river. A stranger, one of the land's random dead. Brains bashed open. That skull like pebbles around a large soft wound or sex. Some mussel a gull dropped on the rocks and lost.
He stood shocked only
that the casement's leaking up
ether was but dull,
having no influence as it left—Sassamon
did not look up but did
mark its direction.

The disoriented intent burst of color & vapor his own observations and imaginings divined must have happened directly at the instant the skull cracked. Next time he would not miss that expression.

THE WORKING, THE LIVING

[Reverend John Eliot: to an English Writer, 1660]

'Sir.

'By reading your book, entitled *Jews in America*, or *Probabilities that the Americans be of that Race*, the Lord did put into my heart to search into some Scriptures about that subject, and by comparing one thing with another, I thought, I saw some ground to conceive, that some of the Ten Tribes might be scattered even thus far, into these parts of America, where we are according to the word of God, Israel shall be brought in by their own covenant, and that the Gentiles shall be blessed, quickened, and brought in by virtue of their coming in . . . And be glad shall he be, that can get hold on the skirt of a Jew, I have some cogitations, as well as others, of the first peopling of America.'

[Eliot: of Sciatic Pain & Paralysis, of the Work, of finding
Sassamon]

Limping August to November,
the condition going over, I set my mind
to a new frame: making the firebrand

God's own hand from hip to toe
showing me to know Him in this burning
numb forerunner of heaven. A missive

only into mine own mind—the seal
inward for no man to see
or them to feel though I am

struck to the ground by it. Such is His call
that our eyes cannot look upon Him,
so this feeble wheel of mine feels

afire from His mere token & reminder: Up,
and be doing, and the Lord will be with thee.
But removing earth's under-pressure
(fallen back in the latitude of dull sleep)

this loving torture abates, leaving me
as a plain man in this world.
To think, to stay speechless, to take

that next step & taste the light
wrought across my very eyes
with the Lord's electric storm

down my right side shaking even
my teeth. My comings & goings
secretly mapped—a geography

of sensation I inwardly diagram
by loving attention—grown of
a sort of metallic hum of empty

pasturage taken up into me: Pain.
I pray heaven shall be similar
but wholly pleasant & populated.

Thus His message is no horses,
walk slow, sit only
with rigid attention, covet not
your body, harvest words & souls only the most light difficult
matter no heavy coarse grain, unwrap every moment from only its
own perception, from its own side, do not make mental construc-
tions of some guessed future when it is only the Lord's unturned
pages writ as the past is writ for what you know not nor should
worry in guessing, love thy wife for she is a helpmeet unto you—
Oh Anne—
in all activity
bend at the knee making
every duty prayer. Do not be
a plain unpained man.

One particular remedy I have found for the insensate uselessness
of the leg is to cinch breeches about that ankle and fill the leg
with nettles. This total attack to the sense of that part appears to
draw down a larger and functioning awareness.
So I become an iatromechanic for the lame conveyance of my own
soul.

And still the work is a continual calling unto me with its signs and provisions, for 'there is also a Blackmoor maid, that hath long lived at Dorchester in New England, unto whom God hath so blessed the public and private means of grace that she is not only indued with a competent measure of knowledge in the mysteries of God, and conviction of her miserable estate of sin; but hath also experience of a saving work of grace in her heart, and a sweet savour of Christ breathing in her' who 'hath with tears exhorted some other of the Indians that live with us to embrace Jesus Christ, declaring how willing he would be to receive them, even as he had received her.'

'God first put into my heart a compassion over their poor Souls, and a desire to teach them to know Christ, and to bring them into his Kingdom. Then presently I found out (by God's wise providence) a pregnant witted young man, who had been a Servant in an English house, who pretty well understood our Language, better than he could speak it, and well understood his own Language, and hath a clear pronunciation: Him I made my Interpreter. By his help I translated the Commandments, the Lord's Prayer, and many Texts of Scripture.

'Also I compiled both Exhortations and Prayers by his help.'

[Anne Eliot: of Eliot, the Work, her Work]

My love for the work and duty
of loving this intrepid limping library
my yokefellow Eliot is too much.
Yet I am a seal to his work,
he says, and take off his secular cares
so that he might fix the hearts
of the Indians etc. A hard morsel to chew,
with domestical duties
soiling what luster wherewith nature's
Nature decks our loving parts.
Our real and most mutual
affection is the minor piece
of his foundation, and yet still more
than I deserve. Even in marriage
we are not let loose to pursue
what brutish pleasures would
toil for at the expense of spirit.
Lord, when will you glue my heart
to God above all things,
above my husband? To stir up
lust for my love of him
is itself effeminate. His strong restraint
and supplication are a saint-like
conformity to our mutual duties,
which want in their muting
of my own forward and frothy thoughts.
His obligation, though, is not my right.
As childbirth gives us
ten months to seek comfort
in Christ if he will take us
to him in death that day, this marriage
is my opening text to eternal
meditations. And the groaning

beer of salvation is more
than yet I taste. Eliot is espoused
first to Christ and reborn through him—
a more motherly birthing
than I ever.
So it is mine
to seek wool and flax,
work willingly with my hands,
lay them to spindle and distaff.
Rising while it is still night
to have the flummery or soft samp
hot for dawn. The fire, the sponge
and barm, are but more children to me,
warming and feeding us lovingly
if I can but attend their continuity
while they try me with their fickles
of tempestuous yeast or simpering
embers. I must bridge dearth
to bounty—bacon flitch in the chimney,
souse in the barrel. If any small
quiet moment creeps to me,
God finds me with a gentle reminder
by the singing of the cider.

[LORD'S PRAYER, Matthew 6: 9-13]

Our father   heaven in   hallowed
'Nooshun   *kesukqut,*   *quttianatamunach*

thy name   come   thy kingdom
koowesuonk.   *peyaumooutch*   *kukketassootamoonk,*

thy will   done earth on
Kuttenantamoonk   *ne n nach ohkeit*

as   heaven in   our food
neane   *kesukqut.*   *Nummeetsuongash*

daily   give   us   this this   day
asekesukokish   *assamaiinean*   *yeuyeu*   *kesukod.*

and   forgive   us   our
Kah   *ahquontamaiinnean*   *nummatch-*

sins   as   wicked-doers
eseongash   *neane*   *matchenehukqueagig*

we forgive   them   also   lead
nutahquontamounnonog.   *Ahque*   *sagkom-*

us   not   temptation in
pagunaiinnean   *en*   *qutchhuaonganit,*

oh   deliver   us   evil
webe   *pohquohwussinnean*   *wutch*

from   for   thine   kingdom
matchitut.   *Newutche*   *kutahtaun*   *ketassootamoonk,*

and	power	and	glory
kah	*menuhkesuonk,*	*kah*	*sohsumoonk*

forever	Amen.
micheme.	*Amen.'*

[Eliot: of Sassamon]

When my young tawny genius here discovered the Greek of it, he so quick taught himself and sketched out an intralineary from pure habit and instinct as we proceeded. I have here at my disposal a mind such not as even the King's Popish scribes can claim. We will do the work, our dual calling.

Lord's Prayer, Sassamon's Greek verbatim:
Thus therefore pray you: Father of us the one in the heavens, let be revered the name of you, let come the kingdom of you, let be done the will of you, as in heaven also on earth. The bread of us daily give to us today. And forgive us the debts of us, as also we have forgiven the debtors of us. And do not bring us into temptation, but rescue us from the evil one.

And then writ for me variants of the opening phrase, which, he says, would be the ideal usages village to village walking from here to the bitter end of the Cape, tongues being refreshed every 40 or 60 miles:

Our father who art in the starry sky
Our father among the great luminaries
Father-heaven
Father-sun-in
He looking down lovingly on many sons
Our father, our sky, you watch us
Son maker by the sun (of the stars)
Starry protector to us
Above earth, from the Southwest, we came as your children

And they say he is simply 'an Indian in the College at Cambridge,'
They say,
'some time he had spent in Preaching the Gospel to Unkus'
'by the Authority of New Plimouth sent to Preach in like manner
      to King Philip'

'an Indian Scholar and Minister'
'spent some years in the Study of Divinity'
'judged capable of Preaching the Gospel'
'a very cunning and plausible Indian'
'did apply himself to preach'
'better gifted than any other of the Indian Nation'
'observed to conform more to the English manners than any other
         Indian'
'report was he was a bad man'
'Philip got him to write his will and he made the writing for a
         great part of the land to be his'

[Grace Indian—a girl]

The girl did not talk. It was an accident to her head. She did hear.
Her tongue was articulate against teeth and mouth but made no
usual sound. Or it was, from her very birth, silent. Or she suffered
some young stroke under the sun of her own accord, or. Or. Or.
Bright. Hands like mother birds in motion keeping eyes off the
open nest her mouth. Mother birds cleaning, feeding the air
around a small brown body.

People think they are silent when they shut their mouths.
But the ocean keeps flowing
against the shore of them. This girl,
Grace Indian, is a seal
unseen in the ocean against their shore.

Food, sleep, attention—her mouth works differently around
these, does not need.

Grace Indian does not speak,
Grace Indian hides corn in the cold fire,
Grace Indian goes swimming,
indicates the air around her face or fingers,
grabs a rifle with both hands from the wrong direction,
ties many many red leaves together and sends them down river to
        bend like a blood-arm over the waterfall,
covers the fire rocks in mud,
weaves green grass around the whole trunk of a birch tree,
attracts always small swarms of children,
makes a headdress of dandelions for the horse,
tries to kill who tries to cut her hair,
covers the floor with cranberries,
rings the firepit with dead butterflies,
closes her eyes and walks across the bridge, forearms level to the
        water, fingers spread,

makes snow with cattail cotton,
writes 'God' on the road to Boston with five dead snakes,
walks English,
stacks 23 shark jaws like hats and fights off all comers,
builds a small Boston of high tide ice,
arrives naked, her dress a sack of oysters,
makes rope from spider webs,
Grace Indian
gets five lashes by King Philip's order.

[English Parliament, 1649]

'Act for the promoting and Propagating of the Gospel of Jesus Christ in New England'

'Whereas the Commons of England assembled in Parliament have received certain intelligence, by the testimonial of diverse faithful and godly Ministers, and others in New-England, that diverse the Heathen Natives of that country, through the blessing of God upon the pious care and pains of some godly English of this Nation, who preach the Gospel to them in their own Indian Language, who not only of Barbarous are become Civil, but many of them forsaking their accustomed Charms and Sorceries, and other Satanical Delusions, do now call upon the Name of the Lord . . . with tears lamenting their mis-spent lives, teaching their Children what they are instructed in themselves, being careful to place their said Children in godly English families, and to put them to English Schools, betaking themselves to one wife, putting away the rest, and by their constant prayers to Almighty God morning and evening in their families . . . it is hereby Enacted by this present Parliament, and by the authority thereof, that for the furthering so good a work, and for the purposes aforesaid, from henceforth there shall be a Corporation in England.'

[Eliot: of The Interpreter]

Thus, Sassamon will be well-used—he sees words.
In the air of it.   To shapechange,
to translate one
or some is simple: breathe
words in, to the meaning
(keeping that inside lungs)
and the tune
(keeping that simply singing)
that another language likes
—this divergent mix enters unto
some obscure process
of organic formation—
and press that out his mouth! This new breath
then fills into the old meaning. Sassamon's position,
in interpreting, is always upwind. This air, these two languages in
two forms moves toward a third. By example, as I understand it, a
body mass of understood English words approaches unto a larger
more constant space of Massachusett "understanding" (itself as
an atmosphere). All this, he sees within his visual consciousness.

The known words drift toward the understanding and, as a tide to
a shore, form to its shape. This visual formation appears to him as
the words interpreted. The sounds interpreted. Though in a way
other than letters. More, I deduce, like a shaped ghost or map of
meaning.

He tells me: *This is simple if you don't stop doing when the papoose is loosened
and you are let out (thinking) into your own breath. We are lazy with what we
think we have and strive always for what is just beyond. Few master even their
immediate surroundings. None do. Your impression on a still day—out of
doors—travels no further than the branches from a small tree's trunk.
See that,* he says, *see what you make on this world.*

Thus, many scenes of desired interpretation have been given over for bad weather, winds, etc. He likes nothing better than a most gentle and constant zephyr. A still day tends to infuriate as a stubborn mule would. Gusting tempests (as do sometimes favor our new coast) put a cold stop to any adventure, even within a good wigwam. These acting, I deduce, like a disappearing of ink or rather a constant hand scraping the slate. Firesmoke is not unpleasant to this miraculous conversation of currents. The proximity of the ocean also being to the liking of Sassamon's genius and skill for some light-giving properties it has for (being reflective under) the low sky we live within.

As I have my light appearing more and more towards the perfect day, he says, so he can hope for "air appearing more and more towards the perfect translation" of that, the Bible of our Massachusett language.

Long after some meeting he interpreted, he may sit there watching the room settle back to its original shape and meaning.

He looks to books because they affect not the air, but also they have none. A thing he desires and fears.

I am working to proceed with his ideas, being as they are a cause or by-product of his particular genius, and only know to start here: Breath indeed is the prayer of a new creature.

Eliot: to the Governor and Commissioners of the Colony

'I shall be put to sundry great charges, and I request that you would please to allow me something towards the same; and the rather I am bold to propose it, because in all the public meetings, motions, journeys, translations, attendances upon the press, and other occasions that I have attended in this work, I have never had (to my knowledge and remembrance) the least acknowledgement from yourselves, or one penny supply, save my bare salary; and I am forced now to move, because I am fallen into debt . . . to beg I am ashamed, and such wants do much hinder me from doing that which otherwise I might do, had I herewith.'

Colony: to Eliot

'How you could mistake our meaning concerning your allowance is yet to us unknown. . . . We still conceive that there are some small difference betwixt Mr. Rawson's account and yours in the tools you received but we put little weight there and marvel how you should think our meaning should be shoes and stockings.'

Eliot: to the Society for the Propagation of the Gospel

'. . . and my requests for some help of some great charges this year; but *they are pleased to answer me with silence, as it is wont to be* . . . and my humble request is that it may be paid, and then I shall be out of debt; but if it should be refused, than *my hands are tied, I can do little; yet I am resolved through the grace of Christ, I will never give over the work so long as I have legs to go.* I am at a dead lift in the work; if the Lord stir up the hearts of men to help me, blessed be his name, and blessed be they that help me; if no man help me.'

Society for the Propagation of the Gospel: to Colony

'Give us leave to tell you there is such a material objection here started as we are ashamed of and know not how to answer, viz. the complaints made by Mr. Eliot to sundry of his friends here that you allow him but £20 per annum which doth not bear his charges in so much as he runs in debt every year more and more and is disabled for giving his children the education he otherwise would. . . . We are far from justifying Mr. Eliot in his turbulent and clamorous proceedings, but the best of God's servants have their failings, and as such we look upon him.'

Eliot: to Colony

'Thus shall I extend so far as I can, but besides, this work of sending forth church messengers is still incumbent upon us; yea, increased much by these stormy times. . . . Captain Gookings will inform you of some charges in powder and shot for their necessary defence in these times of danger.'

[Robert Boyle, scientist and president of the Society: a personal note to Eliot]

Honorable Reverend in Christ,
As we both seek the improvement of souls by our clear faculties I
fear lest our conversation become dull mortal money matters.
Your work is the only answer of truth—and by that I proceed.
You shall be supported. I enclose humble notes toward my latest
work, building from and toward fresh experiments, as I know our
godly educated ministers of New England to be interested what
experience and experiment can deduce of God's many gifts to
us . . .

'Toward a General History of the Air'

'The continual Use of the Air is so absolutely necessary to our
Life, I can scarce think it unworthy to be preserved in Writing. I
freely confess to you, that I much suspect there lies yet something
concealed in it, that needs a further Discovery, which may perhaps
be made by further Trials. In regard that I thought it most
convenient so to contrive my Experiments, as to make such of
them as I could to serve me, both to produce Air, and to examine
it. Of the Structure of the Elastical Particles of the Air, diverse
Conceptions may be framed. . . .'

'The CONTENTS of the several TITLES of the
        History of the AIR.
Title 1. What we understand by the Air
Title 2. Of the constant and permanent Ingredients of the Air
Title 3. Of the Aether in the Atmosphere
Title 4. Of the Springy Particles of the Air, and the Spring of the
        Air
Title 5. Of the Magnetical Particles in the Air
Title 6. Of the Destruction, Generation, Absorption and

[Eliot: handing this note to Sassamon]

I believe I have found a correspondent equal to your inclinations.

[Eliot: of Speaking with the Indians, and Their Questions]

'There is need of learning in Ministers who preach to Indians, much more than to English men and gracious Christians, for these had sundry philosophical questions:
'What was the cause of thunder?'
'Of the Ebbing and Flowing of the Sea? Of the wind?'
'How it comes to pass that the Sea water was salt, and the Land water fresh?'
'Whether Jesus Christ did understand, or God did understand Indian prayers?'
'How come the English do differ so much from the Indians in the knowledge of God and Jesus Christ, seeing they had all at first but one father?'
'When God saith, Honour thy Father, doth he mean three Fathers? Our Father, and our Sachem, and God?'
'Why the English call them Indians, because before they came they had another name?'
'Seeing the English had been 27 years (some of them) in this land, why did we never teach them to know God till now?'
'To what Nation Jesus Christ came first unto, and when?'
'Why did not God kill the Devil that made all men so bad, God having all power?'
'If they leave off Powwowing, and pray to God, what shall they do when they are sick?'
'Before I knew God, I thought I was well, but since I have known God and sin, I find my heart full of sin, and more sinfull than ever it was before, and this hath been great trouble to me.'
'Do not Englishmen spoil their souls, to say a thing cost them more than it did? and is it not all one as to steal?'
'What English men did think of Mr. Eliot because he came among wicked Indians to teach them?'
'How is the tongue like fire, and like poison?'
'I see why I must fear Hell, and do so every day. But why must I fear God?'

'Why did Christ die for us, and who did kill him?'
'Why must we love our enemies, and how shall we do it?'

~~~

'A squaw': 'Whether she might not go and pray in some private place in the woods.'

[King Philip: His Question]

'When the English first came my father was great man and the English as a little child, he constrained other Indians from wronging the English and gave them corn and showed them how to plant and was free to do them any good and had let them have a 100 times more land than now I have for my own people, but my brother when he was king came miserable to die being forced to Court as they judged poisoned'?

[Cartography]

England
Ocean
Ocean
Ocean
Ocean
Ocean
Ocean
Ocean
Ocean
Ocean
Ocean
Ocean
Ocean
Ocean
Ocean
Ocean
Ocean
Ocean
Ocean
Ocean
Ocean
Ocean
Ocean
Ocean
Ocean
Ocean
Ocean
Ocean
Ocean
Beach
Empty Fields
Trees
Forever

[An Indian: of the English]

'What much hoggery, so big walk, and so big speak, and by and by kill.'

[Agreement of Philip and the English, 1662]

'There being occasion of some suspicion of a Plot intended by the Indians against the English, Philip, the brother of the aforesaid Moanam (Alexander), and son of Massasoit, and now the implacable Enemy of the English, make his personal appearance at the Court held at Plimouth, August the 6th; and did there earnestly desire the continuance of that amity and friendship that had formerly been between the Governours of Plimouth and his Deceased Father and Grandfather; and for that end the said Philip doth for himself and his Successors, desire that they might for ever remain subject to the King of England . . . that he will not at any time needlessly or unjustly provoke or raise war with any of the Natives, nor at any time give, sell, or any way dispose of any Lands to him or them appertaining, to any Strangers, or to any without our privity or appointment; but will in all things endeavour to carry it peaceably and inoffensively towards the English.

Witness, John Sassamon
        The Mark of Francis
        the Sachem of Nauset.

The Mark of Philip, alias Metacom'

[A Logick Primer]

'Syllogism
'*Ogusanukoowaonk*

Third   positive   form,   when   both   Propositions   alike
Nishwe   ponamoe   wuttinniyeuonk   neeswe   pakodtittumooongash   netatuppe

begin,   because   the Argument   is the Subject   in   both
kutchissinuhettit,   newutche   wequohtoonk   ne teagoooo   ut   naneese

Propositions:
pakodtittumooonganit.

Some   poor   in this world   shall   be saved   in heaven.
Nawhutche   matchekuog   yeu ut muttaohket   pish   wadchanoog   kesukqut.

The Argument: because   they believe.'
Wequohtoonk: newutche   wunamptamwog.'

38

[Robert Boyle: to John Sassamon]

To my honored new friend, John Sassamon, translator and empiricist

Many thanks for your questions about the method and construction of my experimental machines and measurements. I follow here with my own curiosities, to which I hope to adhere you.

It being the design of the Royal Society, for the better attaining the End of our Institution, to study Nature rather than Books, and the Observations made of phenomena and effects she presents, we think upon and set down some Directions for such Savages amongst the diverse colonies as have been civilized and educated, the better to fit them for making such observations abroad; of which the said Natives should be desired to keep an exact Diary, delivering a fair copy thereof to England. Which Catalogue of Directions having been drawn up; they are such, as follows:

1.   To observe the declination of the Compass, or its variation from the meridian of the place, frequently; marking withal, the Latitude and Longitude of the place, wherever such observation is made, as exactly as may be, and setting down the Method, by which you made them.
2.   To carry Dipping Needles with you, and observe the Inclination of the needle in like manner.
3.   When in your sports, to make faithful record of all particular and remarkable victories, viz., their height, distance, speed, &c. Also the spiritual vigor of the victor, such as you judge.
4.   To remark carefully the Ebbings and Flowings of the Sea, in as many places as you can, together with all the Accidents, Ordinary and Extraordinary, of the Tides. . . .
5.   To send flakings of any precious metals taken, with Latitude, Longitude, and depth of excavation, local dangers & superstitions &c.
6.   To send the bones of any animals unknown to us, or of

remarkable specimens of your enemies, such as giants and famed warriors.

7.   To make Plots and Draughts of prospect of Coasts, Promontories, Islands, and Ports. . . .

8.   To describe the nature and tilt of your women in childbirth and any particularities of practices leading to that state.

9.   To observe and record all Extraordinary Meteors, Lightnings, Thunders, *Ignes Fatui,* Comets, &c. marking still the places and times of their appearing, continuance, &c.

10.   To keep an experimental daily diary of your diet, exertions, and expulsions to send to us.

11.   If possible, and from an enemy, to send a vellum of skin from such inhabitants as can be found farthest north, south, west, and of those common to living at mountaintops.

12.   To send clippings from any plants or animal parts that do affect the minds or perceptive faculties of men.

13.   To tell us where you came from, and how.

[John & John, Working at the Press, Always]

Sassamon: To enter unto Church membership, these Relations of Lord's grace require not the truth?

Eliot: They must be truthful.

Sassamon: Why then some men I have seen telling their truth are turned away?

Eliot: It must be their truth, but it also needs be God's.

Sassamon: Yea, can any man outrun the Lord in truth?

Eliot: Nay.

Sassamon: Well, then.

Eliot: Such men as you have witnessed, and I know them well, being not much affected in their hearts, such is God's mysterious ways, then their truth is only such as they themselves deem it— honestly so—but unredeemed by Christ.

Sassamon: Yet they too are sons of Christ.

Eliot: Truly.

Sassamon: 'Tis an awful business that puts everything into words alone, leaving no meat free from men's mouths. And if the Lord were hungry, he would not tell us, for the world is his, and the fullness of it.

Eliot: Surely some congregations have misjudged in some instances. The safety then is in the great perseverance and terror which is God's gift to his true saints closer to their hearts than mouths. Recall, John, that hunting-fear you told of, which clears your mind and arrow.

Sassamon: In this matter then it is an easier way for the eloquent man of small fire than to be a great mute blaze of grace and faith. This I see without saying or hearing. This is plain to see.

Eliot: 'Tis true men's ears seem wholly given to judgment while our eyes that should see also the carriage of faith and passion are greatly distracted by mere worldly affairs and dangers. 'Tis true.

Sassamon: Gouge my eyes or ears and I will starve. But stop my mouth full of wax before the hunt and truly you will never see such a harvest of deer.

[In such a vein they would work without tire from dawn to the last candle, the Apostle often flat out on his board for God's trial of pain in his leg, handing letters to Sassamon one at a time building the Book of Matthew. Sassamon alone aware of Grace Indian ghosting about and even inside the place.]

[Eliot: Letter to an English Minister, 1668]

'Your question about our Indians is this—*I pray tell me how far that Indian language reacheth which you have translated the Bible, and how numerous their languages are, and what hopes of further success are within your present prospect?*

'Answer.

'For the extent of our Massachusett or Narragansett language (for these are all one). By an eminent providence of God, the extent thereof is very large, though not without some variation of dialect, yet not such as hindereth a ready understanding of each other. And all parts which receive the word of God, and pray, do readily understand the Bible; and these books will be a means to fix, and extend, this language. It is more then a hundred miles eastward from us to Cape Cod, the utmost extent of our Eastern continent near us. All these speak our dialect. Our language is understood Northward as far as Canada. How far Southward I cannot tell.

'The reasons for this wonderfull extent of this language are 3.

'(1) The Massachusetts and Narragansett Sachems have held a very vast imperium over all parts, far and near, as also the Pequots, who are by the Narragansetts, have been great conquerors and rulers' and speak as such their language vastly as civilization had Latin for vast
trade & power, Hebrew
for Divinity—this our Massachusett
then is the very Hebraic Latin
of this new clean wilderness.
'(2) Because the Narraganset Bay is the principal, if not the only place in all this country, where that shellfish is found, of which shells they make their jewels and money of great value, and the royal ornaments—of use and value as far as Mexico.' See the

giant Quahog shell—it is a field of white insides
with one small reserve
of purple—in its scarcity
the meat of value, in its value
the very language—
and in all this I venture
both the size and worth
of this place and Work
to the whole world.

    '(3) By reason of the situation of the countries, butting
upon the Narragansett Bay—the only or principal soil that produces
the money and jewels. By reason of this situation these parts were
places of great resort from all parts and their language desirable—
also, since the English came to these parts, these places are much
resorted unto. Thus, by the overruling providence of God, the
Bible is in the finest language to be spread over all the country'
where they but speak
these trinkets
with the tongue of God
we must enlarge
these original linguists
to their true inheritance. These vowels
have been sowing this soil
for untold centuries—we must
keep their tongue a key
to the reaping thereof. Imagine,
sir, a man praying
a thousand years unawares.
What does God hear? The very word
"wampum" walks the whole
of this new world
as a mouth'd value, so
our Work here will translate
untold spiritual treasures
through our Massachusett *Lingua Umbilicus Mundi*

unto all with ears to hear. All things, sir,
will be outward from here
until the hard bar of eternity
sweeps all up and down.
'The fields are white
but laborers are few. The work
is chargable and full of difficulty,
and few or almost none have an heart
to set upon it. Pray for this day of small things.'

[John Sassamon Sits on the Hill Above Seaport]

observing the efficiencies of conveyance and the future—
communicating itself into the warehouse. These direct movements
toward intended destination create a taste-full pleasure, a
man-made river of movement irrigating by deliberate waters not
waiting for God's rain.

The cargo has made the men muzzled and reined—their languages,
while abundant, are universally tuned toward real action. There is
no translator in the deep hold other than the transfer of things
across a physical space they all see. Their faces only play the
insatiable straight lines of moving merchandise.

Sails break off the not infinite distant horizon and arrive the next
day to break down further into individual boxes that might contain
boxes of very small nails. Sassamon thinks of himself as a nail.
He thinks of a box, and boxes of boxes, and boxes on ships, ships
tilting in the sea.

The horizon: one side-edge of God's cargo box. (*Cargo ball, I pray,* a
sailor tells him.)

The largest crates rest deep in the hold where such extra value is
ballast. They cannot return empty—the ship would capsize. Such
conversing back across the ocean is ruled by improvement or careful
patient waiting silence, coffins hauled from the kelson packed
with rum and tea come for English trade for the living carried in
those boxes that would carry them.

[Co-Signators to Land Transactions Sassamon Brokered, Witnessed, Surveyed, etc.]

Achawanancott

Akoonnumett

Apenumat

Aquetaquish

Ayvanum

Bosworth, Jonathan Senior

Bradford, William

Briggs, Johathan

Browne, James

Browne, John Junior

Cooke, Thomas

Crow, William

Crow, William

Dellano, Johathan

Dennis, Robert

Dennis, Robert

ffrancis Sachem of Nausett

ffrancis Sachem of Nausett

Hawes, Edmond

Hawes, Edmond

Hinkley, Thomas

Hinkley, Thomas

Kaley, Micaell

Lydly, Thomas

Mackacom

Mamanawatkey Sachem of Saconett

Mannanwoke

Momonway

Morton, Nathaniel

Naneheunt

Nelson, William

Nelson, William

Nesetaquason

Old Watuspaquin

Pamatacom

Papamok

Papanoe

Paquonack

Paventeakanaet

Paventeakanoet

Penichason allis Nimrod

Philip ye Sachem

Phillip

Phillip

Phillip

Phillip

Phillip Sachem

Phillip Sachem

Phillip the Sachem

Phillip the Sachem

Phillip the Sachem

Phillip the Sachem

Phillipe

Pompaquase

pomvitchawshoant

Sampson

Sampson

Sansannowaskon

Sassamon, Rowland

Sassamon, Rowland

Showamsett

Southworth, Thomas

Southworth, Thomas
Sprague, Samuel
Squamett
Stanford, William
Tabor, Thomas
Taquanksitke
Tatapanum
Thomas the Indian
Tisdall, John
Tokomomock
Totmonna
Tupaquin, William
Uskowantoson, Capt.
Ussamequin
Wadsworth, Christopher
Wamssita alias Alexander
Wamusutta
Wamusutta
Watapatakne
Weropatokin
Wewoosken
Willett, Thommas
Winslow, Josiah
Winslow, Josiah
Winslow, Josias
Winslow, Nathaniel
Winslow, Nathaniel
Wootonekanuske

[Eliot Reads Psalms to Sassamon]

who sings them almost simultaneously back in another tongue
suddenly reaching right into Eliot's mouth to reshape *"shiggaion"*
for him:

> Shiggaion of David, which he sang unto the Lord, concerning
> the words of Cush the son of Benjamin.

> *Shi-gah-yoneh!*

The scrape of hunter's hands on his tongue shocking the Reverend
into an instant vision of sitting in Israel, hearing her true song.

His joy at this vision, immense—but not of a quality to allow
Sassamon's attempt to correct *shiggaion*'s air currents with direct
intervention of one mouth's lesson upon his. He understood the
immediate and fruitful importance of such translation and
pronunciation, but was also certain the Lord would provide
avenues more seemly than kissing words back and forth.

[Sassamon: of Communication]

One word becomes another by suffocation across whatever is the
virgin, inviolable concept. One wallowing becomes another
wallowing—the way men will die the same but make different
noises to do it. Guttural resistant clicks or that nice rounded
resignation, blood and meaning pool in the throat to push out
pure air. The birds and animals don't word, don't talk of death.
Void themselves of their young, lick the blood, move food to
mouths without hands. Another difference between us and them
is glass. You can see through the hole you cut to pull the guts out
will be where you slip inside them for warmth.
For you've made a coat of the world's parts.
There are animals larger than any man.
Trees, and projections of earth.
We take one step back
and lay a little word
to each thing. Lay our mouth on it in a layer
and say it to others who don't ever remain silent so the wood
becomes full of such half-sense—the gutted and cured hides of
our minds draped over everything that ignores cold and snow.
Suffocating. When summer runs long I hide on the island for days
to gather distance and then swim into it and cry like an English
woman dying just to be alive in one real moment of silence.
Finding great relief each year in my surprise that this simple and
deliberate mechanism remains effective.
I come ashore and return to work.

[Sassamon: Letter to Boyle]

Sir, I am pleased to supply observations requested. Set my braves and agents to work in collecting them. Having occasion, I thought to supply you current theories about healthfulness and insalubrity of the Air of our land among English in hopes you design some tests of experiment for them in ways you did set forth.

In diverse of Cases I see no Cause to happy Constitution may more be ascribed, than friendly Effluvia sent up from Soil; which Particles, either promoting transpiration or mortifying and disabling some noxious Particles that would otherwise infest Air, may contribute to keep Bodies of those English in that regular and desirable state you call Health. It is probable in diverse places some Endemical English Diseases do mainly, or at least part depend upon Subterraneal Steams.

Conversely, one season of first English air to spill from sails here killed ten thousand Indians within a day's walk from mine own dead parents.

Particles not only affect human bodies as taken in Respiration, but as outwardly touch Skin: and Skin being pierced full with Pores, as you have wisely shown, and those in different sizes and figures, Corpuscles that get in may have operation, even upon inward parts of a body. You have also seen how words breathed in particular way make some men mad unto murderousness. Words, as pores, have different figures.

May there not be an alphabet of pores?
The vulgar elements of atmosphere get entrance at numerous Orifices of miliary glandules of Skin, or other places. One stops up ears not only to avoid noise, but what it carries along on and with. Communication has its many meanings and misses.

If I had leisure, and thought necessary, I could show great many odd and surprizing things to be met with in the Structure (as Scripture) of parts of Earth that lie but a little way beneath surface. Even such as make communication in tongues most impossible, and there be not light for reading.
The certain hell of being misunderstood.

But the Devil revels in such bad air. Which by Wind hurried along, and blown against Bodies stood in its way, like Hail-shot discharged out Gun, here in closer, and there more scattering order . . . Such as I show occurs with dispersal of our spoken words or poison dust upthrown. One needs only lash a man to one tree and walk up wind.

Please send diagrams and animadversions, each I will instantly apply. I am at service to such sciences as you serve.
—John Sassamon, Translator

[Eliot: of Indian Sounds, of Mankind]

'Musical sounds they also have, and perfect Harmony, but they
 differ from us in sound.
There be four several sorts of Sounds or Tones uttered by Mankind.
1.   Articulation in Speech.
2.   Laughter.
3.   Laetation and Joy: of which kind of sounds our Music
        and Song is made.
4.   Ululation, Howling, Yelling, or Mourning: and of that
        kind of sound is their Music and Song made.'

[John & John, At the Press, Always]

They had a game.

Tell Me of Your People's Wisdom.

Its provenance and evolution lost in their long play and hours of workplace talk, a gag, really, that Sassamon played on Eliot out of boredom. Talking nonsense, mocking the old drunk Indians down at the seaport selling fake trinkets and myth to green sailors for a cup of grog. Until Eliot saw the gag coming one day and decided to play at it straight, to play along: *Tell me, Chief Sassamon, about your people's great wisdom,* he said.

Many moons ago, Sassamon began (always began, and then it was never once the same spun yarn): many moons ago, long before Great Black Beaver Eliotonkinamus and Mother ocean joined in the river galaxy to birth Massachusett Land, my people lay in the earth as stones—silent & wise & awaiting the river time.

One day, Great Beaver Eliotonkinamus came limping along the beach and Mother Ocean said, *Let us be married and do married things tonight!* But the diligent Beaver only frowned, for he had much work to do. He was building a dam out of paper so he could invent rivers to carry his beaver coats to port and then on across Mother Ocean to fine French ladies to wear for the Pope in his palace when all the beaver coats would shit at once. And my people the stones lay silent & wise awaiting Rivertime.

Mother Ocean was determined. The next day she said, *Oh wise Beaver, you want to invent rivers, and I am water herself, the mother of all water. If we marry, I will bear many rivers for your children.* Beaver replied, *Leave me be, Ocean, and do not lap your warm waves so gently against my tail any longer. You are salt water! Where beaver coats will die! I must get back to work on my paper dam. I will add ink to it to help catch the Great Rains between you and*

54

my pond to invent rivers. And my people the stones lay silent & wise awaiting more of this great tale.

And the wisdom of my people slept for a thousand years, Sassamon said, which meant he was stuck for more story. And he'd work in silence for awhile, mock-stoic.

But Mother Ocean was determined to do married things to Eliotonkinininiminusoo, so the next day she said, *Oh wise Beaver with your handsome and firm tail, you need to invent rivers with freshwater to come to seaport. I invite your pond to enter into me and by this you will invent rivers.* Beaver replied, *Leave me to my work, Ocean. You will swallow my pond whole, as you swallow the rain, as the fire swallows the branch, and then the whole earth will be saltwater and I will have to live in your Wigwam forever. I need my own wigwam, with paper & ink & beaverbibles & freshwater.* And my people the stones lay silent & laughing. And wise. Very wise.

But Mother Ocean was like a great moose in rutting season in a full and ripe berry bush with a raven on one horn and an eagle on the other talking birdtalk about the wisdom of my silent stone people, so the next day she said, *Oh diligent Beaver with your beautiful teeth, great inventor of rivers that still do not exist, I will send a good hurricane to embrace your pond and make you my husband forever in a brackish land while the Pope bedevils fine French ladies in his palace wearing Dutch micecoats that do not shit at once but only leave small polite pellets at various hours that bother no one entranced by the great gold and silver palace of the Pope.*

Beaver was about to reply when he was interrupted by the stone people.

In their great wisdom, my people had heard enough of Mother Ocean and Great Beaver Eliotunk-tunk. They broke their wise silence to call their wise brother, the silent moonstone in the sky. They said, *Oh wise silent Brother Moonstone, Mother Ocean must marry Great Beaver, but her saltwater is greedy and dangerous. Please pull her back from the Beaver pond every day and every night so that his beaver coats do not die, and so that he may live in his own Wigwam & work & work. But let her also back in every day and every night, so that she may demand married things from Beaver. It is best.*

Such is the great wisdom of my people: the creation of the tides, the invention of rivers of trade, a happy ocean and busy beaver, the Pope covered in good Massachusett shit. No?

Eliot laughing demurely for whole minutes forgetting his leg pain. A thing no English ever saw.

[Grace Indian, in English dress,]

hard shoes, bonnet,
face: Walking English down Boston's main street. Put a doe in
English clothes and send her to tea, unnoticed. No wonder they
starve. She carries a basket of cormorant eggs. She has buried her
bones to dull the moves. But she has no audience but the ones
there that know nothing of it. Gestures and hesitations scored in
her mind. Watch: when the man approaches, her slightest stumble:
their talk falls to grunts, queer smiles, a tipped hat. Takes people and
changes them in her blood—then simply moves that outward back
to them. People don't see people as much as what they think. She
could walk out from under a starving privateer by accommodating
his assumptions. The street clears. Horse noises and patter move
off-stage now. She stays. In character. Prays silently for some
white wish to keep the rhythms right. Longs for England, an
island. Clucks at the stockades. Watch: she sells the eggs to the
chicken stand without opening her mouth, without lying.

(The one thing she can't do right is cry. The sobs choke horribly
on her clean throat—horrible but wrong. That would be her
safety net here, but she walks the tightrope of main street anyway
without that feminine English defense.)

She is trying to figure
why they always stay with a street once it is made by the things
around it. Why the wearing it out makes them like a place better,
piling higher with boxes and mud and firewood taken from
further and further away. The street feels like the church in its old
worn brownness. Feels like one of seaport's big ships had been
unfolded and laid down here. Is a ship one English town rolled up
and caulked sea-tight? At the end of the street she turns around
like the sunrise and does it again. Fresh scene, new players, the day
is moving. She winds the clock of it with her progress. Practice.

Whose dress is this?

The last thing she does is _____, and
they do not see her depart.

The English cannot see her.
The Indians see her.
Philip hates her unpatterned
all too visibility.

[Eliot: of Sassamon]

Sassamon walks in and nails the seal of the colony to the wall of
the printshack:

'Come over and help us.'

Acts 16.9 'And a vision appeared to Paul in the night; There stood
a man of Macedonia, and prayed to him, saying, Come over into
Macedonia and help us.'

Underneath, with a piece of charcoal, he sketches another Indian.
Picking up my Greek, he makes a banner over his head in the
original text:
Δταβας εις Μακεδουιυ βοηθησου ημιυ

(Oh, If every Harvard boy had such a mind and eye, we would be
a country. We would be Israel, we would make a commerce with
the world in spiritual things.)

He is looking at me, waiting not wanting, I guess, to be a tutor to his tutor. It is a question—his palms at his sides slowly opening in my direction—as much as an accusation, so I say it, I translate literally the written Holy word of our apostle Paul, the words of the man praying to him in sleep, the words of his vision of such, saying: *Having passed over into Macedonia, help us.*

TO GATHER A CHURCH

[John & John, At the Gathering of the Praying Indian
Congregation at Natick, Confessions to Be Heard, 1654]

Sassamon:

English standing around upright on the earth as if everything had
already occurred. I made my eyes the local horizon line and looked
into it: the underair was in eddies from the heads of children. Indian
kids, only. Adults gathering for the interview but with a new difference
in the difference of Indians. I thought it preparation because the air
did have that soft feel of good insistence. My eyes were thinking there;
then—the buck flushed.
A near-white buck flushed from the treeline in two bounds to the center
of town.
The humans all stopped breathing on a short intake.
He released his nostrils. Eyes pinned and resigned. Emptying out the
warm flavor of his mistake into a well of dull men, huffing at the end
of it like a king handing over his head.

Then he wasn't dead.
The in-breath filled his whole head. As translator, I will say his one
more still breath was a bored laughing at us and he walked on, easy
as a cow.

Indians lined up on one side of the street across from the English.
This deer walked right down the seam of the imbalance. I felt the
English rigid flutter, how they will waver into stillness like the Bibles
clutched harder to their hearts had run aground. In such an instant,
while English timbers still ashiver, I have seen every single brave
draw, nock, and let fly an arrow. That day all the Indian muscle
untangling under the too much touch of cloth. Untangling out
toward execution movement. But then held there by 1] their hours
of study, 2] the unsurety of God's will in such meat-luck, and 3] a
kind of shyness before the English and their low regard for natural
reaction. (I doubt not now that some of the older Indians thought

the buck might be God.)

Some collaborations don't come to the usual climax, the flying arrow and animal soliloquy. This cold moment cut instead the throat of mine own soul. I saw that God had been telling our story to us all along, and that the learning of it affected not one part (beyond the single grain of our dull minds) and that the English existed in a separate similar ignorance: a kind of mere owning of the world we walk through.

I looked in his eyes, the buck, and it was a waterfall with us. He walked off domesticated with my old dull frame. I stayed, alive in his wild skin.

So the deer lived. His haughtiness turning to bewilderment, his pulse not slowing but trading its intent. The quick juice of his blood still running but without ignorance. We all stood there—defeated, disarmed. No metaphors. No slump of meat to the earth. No dusty thump of deer freed from itself. We all stood there selfish hiding in unmotion and silence wishing life would go away in the fullness of its sinful opportunities. And still, there was the test we had all come to take.

First buck on this earth to live past the treeline of a Massachusett camp.
I know there is a bottle of rum that arrived simultaneously with this new way of thinking.

The white buck walked out southwest under the white sway of an old ash's glow-shadow. The last place any sighted sane animal would hide.

A Montauk boy and Basque sailor had the bottle hidden behind the third big tree. Baby birds thrust forth their open mouths on stretching necks, screaming, for something to be placed inside them—you can do for them with your fingers—they do not wait for their proper mother and die. If I threw my head back and scream it would be cause for commotion (and probably some English needing to clean his britches). If I stop my mouth with that bottle, it's God's business and fingers. The earth asked for its oceans and Noah eventually came ashore. Some old cuz of mine, John says.

We were busy waiting to be knowledgeable and be humbled.
We waited. John always arriving at 'God's good time,' which is lately and after much idle time unto the faithful.

Eliot:

A wonderful providence today at Natick: a majestic pale buck appeared in the street, seeming to approve and improve us all with Nature's own knowledge of God, and all agreed, English and Indian, that it was some divine blessing. It was much reassuring to me as a light and precursor, some encouragement before God's fuller test, which was this:

Of those to gather, 'three of them had gotten several quarts of Strong-water, (which sundry out of a greedy desire of a little gain, are too ready to sell unto them, to the offence and grief of the better sort of Indians, and of the godly English too) with these liquors, did not only make themselves drunk, but got a Child of eleven years of age, the son of Toteswamp.

'The Tidings sunk my spirit extremely, I did judge it to be the greatest frown of God that ever I met withal in the work, I could read nothing in it but displeasure, I began to doubt our intended work: I knew not what to do, the blackness of the sins and the Persons reflected on, made my heart fail me: For one of the offenders (though least in offense) was he that hath been my Interpreter, whom I have used in Translating a good part of the Holy Scriptures; and in that respect I saw much of Satan's venom, and in God I saw displeasure.

'For this and some other acts of Apostacy at this time, I had thoughts of casting him from that work, yet now the Lord hath found a way to humble him. But his Apostacy at this time was a great Trial, and I did lay him by for that day of our Examination, I used another in his room. Thus Satan aimed at me in this very miscarrying.

'They judged the three men to sit in the stocks a good space of time, and thence to be brought to the whipping-Post, & have each of them twenty lashes. The boy to be put in the stock a little while, and the next day his father was to whip him in the School, before the Children there; all which Judgment was executed.'

Sassamon:

Locked thus in the stocks
is the inescapable exhalations
your body makes you make. The breeze brings you
whatever you will breathe and talk. Triangle of face and hands. You
can imagine a nose itch—but that does not touch the lungs or touch
existence. Can you imagine a futile resistance against not being able
to resist. Where does that exist. Where are God's own breaths. A
collar of oak choking my throat. Throttled by a tree. A pressing just
preliminary to my lungs—I'd be a bellows of woodflesh—gutbag
with a mouth for a mouth to pour out and in from. This tree making
a border between my mind and its bag of piss, air, and shit behind.

Some boys scattered birdseed on me and the finches came to eat and
flutter me small oarstrokes of air. I swallow one whole to get that

wing-freedom inside. I say so, out loud: *the elaboration of language into God's Creation, real imagination, is more complicated than making new life by consummation or consumption.*

Consume this, says a boy smearing shit on my face with a stick.

By flexing my wrists fast the fingers spread some relief toward the face like syllable whispers.

Stuck here sucking myself out of the world and spitting myself back in. Fish-stuck, bird-buried. And blood or whatever lives inside me bubbling at the lips beak lips—can't test it with my fingertips or even properly taste what's too close without hands.

We are contained. The winter toad traps itself mud-deeper than the reach of ice, but above anything else. Above what. Our containers only need one side at a time to keep us in. The earth has one floor. The jailhouse is whichever wall you stare at and another holds you up. We are between and words our temporary traps to keep meaning here. Not being able to bear the responsibility of wavering bodies, to be.

The Natick air entered me. I became mere English bellows, entered into, exited. God drew me open there, as a way to keep my meat alive—mere mortal breathing—but I was just a static gutbag, collecting whatever silt and sediment. Filtering the worst of that town. Children threw brown molasses behind me. Women broke the wet emotion of their eyes, alone—my restraints unconstraining them. Three days English arrived to that Indian town to see my inconvenience, to see my soul's forced fast before the feast of lashing. To cram their air in me so to see it leave when the skin opened.

Picnics. And their words. Even the seaport has its silences. But this crowd dips its dumb noise in me body-deep. Three days the vibrations went endless. Where is it like this on earth. I saw their round faces controlling and becoming some mechanism, some incessant noise toward a separate end. The words were cause and by-product, fuel to my filling up with them, but not anything in themselves. Words had fetched them here and words they spent on me—that's it. That is it. They were a mechanism for what was expected.

But then oh sweetness of the Lord Grace Indian was arrived and revealed to me by Walking English through the whole throng, dropping her stiff dress and bonnet to the ruined earth around us, skin covered in light skin threw her long tent hair over our heads and stood firm against my face all night. They'd have paid money for that, paid dearly, and they don't dare come near it. Just stare. Get what they want without getting any more of me—she is a smart one and directly her air unarticulates my insides. I see her big knife tucked to thigh skin and breathe to her no no no I love you just let them to do. There is no death here.

(night) Sassamon:

Strange night, this conscience, an uncomfortable consequence of a minor change to the structure. Strange system, the consciousness, a symptom of the night. How a man changes by dissipating accumulations. A baiting of the trap with monads of air a mechanical and frictive presence, energy barrier, equilibrium tipped toward the inside. Words are steam leaving the heated gourd. Pop and sizzle of a pumpkin in the fire. Nonuniform bubbles of expansion into every cavity and muscle, every unknown toe and hairtip, a transparent hand and again again it enters actually in any perceived moment digging through me. Matter consumed produces me, my energy. And shit. And words. O God I say as they say their way, and wait. We spread the shit and words over the field before leaving for the season. The English stay. Houses born deformed, too heavy and legless. Inside them the red inside of a woman's mouth makes warmth and wet. Woman, distract and abstract my tongue as it leaps and leaps trying to leave me. Swarmed by grains of what pulls over it in every breath. A retch. A tip of saliva drips to the floor of the mouth. I'm translating with it. My lungs bellow of imperative tense, the forgiving tense, sends exact air currents over the liquid inside me, shaping it. A structured system of spit gathers from the wet between air and sound. Every second requires cerain amounts of spittle in certain spaces and the certain play of air tides it distinctly. My tongue listens in Grace Indian's mouth to the shapewords she won't let leave me.

And she scratched my nose, God bless her.

Eliot:

'When they came to be whipped, the Constable fetched them one after another to the Tree (which they make use of instead of a Post) where they all received their Punishments.' 'The Rulers spake thus, one of them said, *The Punishments for sin are the Commandments of God, and the work of God, and his end was to do them good and bring them to repentance.*

'And upon that ground he did in more words exhort them to repentance, and amendment of life. When he had done, another spake unto them to this purpose, *You are taught in Catechism that the wages of sin are all miseries and calamities in this life, and also death, and eternal damnation in hell. Now you feel some smart as the fruit of your sin, and this is to bring you to repentance, that so you may escape the rest.* And in more words he exhorted them to repentance.

'When he had done, another spake to this purpose, *Hear all ye people* (turning himself to the people who stood round about, I think not less than two hundred, small and great) *this is the Commandment of the Lord, that thus it should be done unto sinners; and therefore let all take warning by this, that you commit not such sins, least you incur these Punishments.* And with more words he exhorted the People. Other of the Rulers spake also, but some things spoken I understood not, and some things slipped from me: But these which I have related remained with me' as he let the lash slip its restful coil. And with zeal in his application of the correction.

Sassamon:

hear all
ye hear
sin
all
are
all

miseries
calamities
you are taught
now you feel
some
do some good
thus it should be done
some good
punishments
good
commandments
warning wages
take wages
the work of God
least you incur
that so you may escape
some smart fruit
of you
unto the rest
His end hear
hear
hear rest
may rest
may escape

Whatsoever, it's written on me now.　　　All this noise let out
from me, a shitbag.

Red spittle shaping its meaning on me

　　　　　　　　　　　　　　without me—pulsing
out my back shaping the crowd gasp and to understand without my
lungs or tongue. English Indian Idiot Minister each hearing the

means by some direct revealing to their consciousness whatever the Lord made upon them. Such terror opens these little red fleshgates of hell on me, open and ignite my brown kindling skin to a dripping blaze—fire falling to the earth from spine and ribroots. Blood translating dust to mud, listening.

I could teach a bear
to fear a flower by these means
this necessary moment
making toward conversion is terror of conscience. Beargod, flowergod, feargod, wisdomgod ofgod mygod my people. *Ordo salutis,* let me arrow loose.

This steam of human innards released has a certain smell—a sperm mild manure of upward motion—whose word currents develop relative to the wound's opening—you need a mortal-sized exposure to find any profound expression of utterance evaporating above the body. Daily we piecemeal this our profundity out in little niggardly breaths and abrasions, words and superficial wounds oh well on the way to a duller, distant death. Ticks sense these gentle outfluxes of use and crawl toward them. I saw the devil in a tick sucking on a tick sucking on my loins.

In what manner shall we trade & interpret blood? In what manner shall we what?

They love best the African for laying on such red text against a darker backpiece but Indian skin being an acceptable such vellum and even occasionally a nice white page not too richly is written the sins of its own story to press against a bed. Printing in one's slumber, hag-written! John would find such a thing greatly efficient.

Once the perception is initiated, there is something of God to be sorted out. These prayers upward without me. Their ink drips in the

dust. Off me. My blood. Without me. Walk free out from under
all.

Not them.

Not anyone.

Not Grace.

I perhaps I will
get down on my knees
and pray. I'll fall
on my face.

[He rose from the ground and walked out southwest under the white
sway of an old ash's glow-shadow. The last place any sighted sane
animal would hide.]

Eliot:

At the old ash, he reached up and behind as if for an arrow and
drawing instead blood from his back made the sign of the cross on
that ancient white wood—how the crowd roared, like a rogue wave
meeting the permanent shore. And then came an ocean of silence
so flat you'd think it fit to uphold your feet. But no one else moved
with anything I'd call intention.
He walked on.
He is gone.

[John dreams/John dreams]

I adjusted my lungs and felt directly my tongue and asked, is there a Word which is the beginning? and didn't know what to answer, so I adjusted the tongue and asked myself, is there God, which is a being or entity, which is more than the Word, which or who, that actually exists? and pushed the tongue away from me, then pulled it in, asking, is there a supreme being, a hearing of prayers, is there a reception of the Word? and twisting the tongue toward my own ear, is there a beginning here? rapping the tongue on teeth and cheek close the ear, or what is called God, or what some call God, who actually Words my hearing here, actually existing up in the air? and did not answer to turning the tongue and tuning the ear higher, then turned them too far, and then one more time back again, is there a beginning to God, an existence outside the Word, or the Word itself somehow not as or more than I know it, does something exist? am I hearing anything, but did not answer again, because I don't know the answer, can't hear it, and pushed the tongue out until it hurt and dried, then I could not talk, but asked, can you hear this Word, can this unbegun beaten tongue speak a Word of God, who exists and somehow is supreme and definitely hearing in existence, a real thing but does not answer always, but I didn't know what to answer, and turned the ear past silence until the air hurt, and back again to regular silence, is there a God, and biting the tongue, and tasting the sound of until I said a yes, a yes I heard and boxed the ear you liar you goddamned liar you and and did you fucking answer me did you yourself think that you were something saved and received in hearing and unlike some others and I was so relieved that I was asked something I knew the answer to that I heard yes, yes, I was the one, I had such sin, yes, I am the one.

[Boyle: to Sassamon]

'I shall offer to your Consideration the Accidents that often happen to Men, by the mere Air, as Convulsions, Cramps, Blastings, Lameness, Colds, many of which indure a Man's Life-time; and which (with many bitter Infirmities that sometimes seize upon a Man, while standing, walking, or lying in the Air) are rarely or never felt or discerned at the Instant of their Approach or Insults upon a Man.

'Wherefore the Air, being a Body so important in our Speculations of Nature, and so necessary to the Continuance of our Lives, I could not but think it deserv'd, that we should solicitously inquire, whether it may or may not be produc'd by Art; for if it can be so by any, not very uneasily practicable ways, the Discovery may not only help us to explicate some difficult Phenomena of Nature, but may afford us, among several other Uses, that of enabling us to supply diverse, if not also submarine Navigators with fresh Air produced under Water, and thereby lengthen their staying in Places, where the Continuance of it may be of great Use both speculative and practical.'

TO COCKENOE'S ISLAND

[And so you walk, Sassamon,]

you walk. Away. All the way
escaping out
into the ocean
where it's still
silent
        and what flies
under
doesn't flutter
frantic
you walk out. All the way out. Escaping from under their air—to
the ocean. Get out the sky. Onto the ocean. Into, out of.
Borrow a small dugout down the river down the shore, walk across
the cape, another boat, down Narragansett waters into Paumanok
Sound to Cockenoe's island at Norwalk. Seven days and nights
without stopping. The moon cresting over full, some brief aware-
ness, well-lit dark of deepnight.

A small island at the head of Norwalk, just out the Saugatuck
River. On a clear day, down the Sound, you can see the land pinch
to New Amsterdam. Here, what English there are are disorganized
and interested only in trade—and Cockenoe brokered them a
good land deal. So you will be left alone to his island, just a rocky
sandbar with a few trees. But clams aplenty in the shallows that
join the island to the neck that forms the harbor. Lobster lying
about half-asleep. These shallows warmed in the sun at low tide
and you lie there, head propped on a rock leaving the ears under-
water.

Sleep like that, leaving the sense of touch and hearing underwater,
closing the eyes and mouth off, smelling the ocean filling the ears,
you sleep using breath only as it was intended for—breath. Barely
that.

At dawn
the leaves and oysters let themselves
open from peace
to fury—the roar of land and ocean
and sun rubbing some warmth up.

The flat tension of earth's wet rolling

And how has it come about
that more than six or seven colors
require your attention, that all
the old words begin to vibrate and steam
upward from where they had settled into it.
The undimmed fullness of the morn and a thousand
new sounds crowding into the irradiated currents—
then, you see, everything
should fold into the singular
essence of what it was
just a second ago in the sun. Good morning,
cormorant, you one tuned
to cruise currents
into silence, whispering
only *fish fish fish*
that's all you need
to resurface.
When the bud of it is gone, the day full open all over you. The
sun comes over the horizon like a ship that now sits dull and
obviously over us drowned by blue.

[Winter passes, and a winter.]

The point of the training is to remain underwater. The point is to remain.

If you find heaven under there, you will first experience it in fleeting only ached moments. But you can train yourself slowly to remain longer without that which keeps you out of heaven. And, like the Grampus, you need only rise briefly into hell for a breath. And with keeping the ears out of the air. Just lungs lifting upward, eyes closed.

Under. Water.

Move. Slow. Sound.
The porpoise are hawkfish soaring into under silence. Think hawk, float, don't talk, tapping beach stones beneath you deeper. Click click sea hawks soaring, click click saying a wet hello to eggs so soft and shell-less delicate, fish live and swim off in a silent substance that endlessly coughs you upward, foreign infection in the earthlung, calls you out upward, sung from a different surface—
unprofundis—
shallow and loud,
floundering,
awkward against their
soaring, their squawks
that call clear miles
through thick
embracing silence
without even wind, barely
existence. That first war,
you watched good Christian men

adhering to such death requests
from their enemies left unransomed.
Better to send any of us to God
by merciful Christian hand
than released grinning
heathens, Eliot said.
And it seems an idea
born out
both by Scripture and the mouth
of the seaport
that has told no lie
since beginning time—tide
comes in, tide goes out—
now it opens wide
to eat what English
ships bring and speaks back
English things
in such solid boxes,
such organized outward utterance,
without one word
of the way it was
before. The sea bears
such horrible truths
honestly and fine, and you
have been an orphan
left by earth
and unwelcomed
to air.

Then:

A great fat Grampus grounded

on shore after that storm. Her mouth
grim and distant from where she breathes—
a fist-size hole fashioned with fishleather flap as a kind of ancient
second mouth remaindered atop the brain. Sense expresses itself,
expires, while keeping the sea from sinking the black cavity. Salt
water around the head seeps somewhat through the cranial plates
to meander and bathe the crevices of the brain, dissolving in its
course all the speaking from the coils to say itself in a fine bursting
mist above the brain. Thus their language is not set loose but falls
back into the belonging sea to remain misunderstood to us. You
dive into its vibrations, trying to lie your body out like the long
swamped canoe of the Grampus, grazing the sandy cradle of the
sea, you are a pocket opening upward in her wet language.

You sit on the sand first, as you've learned to do, with gaze locked
into the water—allowing the oxygen inside to settle like silt. A
raised chamber of water, this body, in which air is but an agent
and cause of agitation. Remove the motion and madness—sit—
then slip your own smooth ocean into the ocean.

You can stay under. You have mastered a full change of shadows
without coming back into the sun.

She is a long beast, and calm—her body a greased gravity that
pulls you along without effort. The sun and remnant life on the
blubber make a slimy cocoon of warmth that draws you in,
breathes you. Muscles run man-length many times from armfin to
tail, whose last twitch leverages a large surge—going over the top,
you are lifted within a significance of water well above the beach
and in that bubbled instance see two more snuffing Grampuses
nudging the sandbar. And her tail draws you back down.

Settling at the other eye, right shoulder anchoring into the sand, left hand caressing the heft that rolls like a whole ocean away and against you, making the giant eye gently *yes, yes, yes* a connective indwelling her heart bigger than your head—and its beat wraps in your being as it slows into the quiet gaps between elaboration, her heart as your own cheek belly thighs tide against her beats less and less-you're-dead and the direct revelation arrives within that, yes, into her eye wholly, you can stay under the ocean & stay & stay so she rolls pinning your right leg inside the soft bottom—the heft and warmth of this God tucking you to bed to pour her ocular knowledge in your head—not a rapture, but the bathing immensity you've known and ignored—not a departure, an awakening and in the closing circles of plain consciousness arrives what the eye is— the expanding darkness all white and the pupil shrinking out the blindness of mere life—body gone, going from fingertips inward—awareness bursts open, thrust from a cliff to immerse into the very sun floating rising & just as your shoulders dissolve, a vast shudder—the giant eye flares with war she shifts & lifts away in new redness & something rips you out by the scalp.

On the beach. The goddammed air, covered in blood, coughing it
out. In your first breath. Fifty grampus aground on the island.
Each with an English or three flaying the blubber from her still-
live eyes.
The water sloshing red loin-deep.
The air clutters with good commerce. With fat smoke.
With this work.

RETURN

[Eliot takes Sassamon back at the printing press]

with this covenant: live simply, preach at Natick, nothing more
than weak beer, give up chasing God between every blasted word
He is there everywhere anyway.
Convert Philip.
Marry that girl.
'The longer I live, and the more experiences I pass through, the
more need I see and feel of a bearing, forbearing, longsuffering,
and when all that is done, of an open cordial loving spirit,
carriage and acting in things. One point of self denial is to deny
ourselves for peace sake.'

[Eliot: to Sassamon—Instructions for Proofing]

1. For each marking-up a distinct mark is to be made:
   (a) in the text: to indicate the exact place to which the instruction refers;
   (b) in the margin: to signify or amplify the meaning of the instruction.

2. Where a number of instructions occur in one line, the marginal marks are to be divided between the left and right margins where possible, the order being from left to right in both margins

3. Specification details, comments and instructions may be written on the copy of proof to complement the textual and marginal marks. Such written matter is to be clearly distinguishable from the copy and from any corrections made to the proof. This is done by encircling the matter and/or by the appropriate use of colour (as below)

4. Proof correction shall be made in coloured ink thus:
   (a) printer's literal errors marked by the printer for correction: green;
   (b) printer's literal errors marked by the translator for correction: red;
   (c) alterations and instructions made by the Reverend: black or blue

Amen

[Sassamon: of Printing the Bible]

The pages indeed require a new attempt at binding by us.
We have not made something
this big, never yet everything.
The binding in-lightens the Word
into word order, His order, *Ordo salutis*. The Old Testament three
years in the press my arm cranking the devil's arm over and down
pressing paper ink metal for three years. We have smoothed over
the imposing stone with our endless literal sweat. Our bled letter'd
fingertips. The inkballs making ink seemingly from their swinging
through air—I can see the entire Bible writ there in reversed
letters.

At night my eyes close backward
on verse I sleep
outside myself for looking back
down upon 'p' & 'q'
upon me as I hope the Lord
reads what's impressed
into my very vision.

Hand-justified, writ out from one pen with my complete input,
each letter set after getting clean in my ear air eye as Eliot reads
aloud.

I dream: inside shut covers the volume of it is His eternal void &
ocean the words swim meaning endlessly and then—we open it—
and His divine direction falls the words to our senses.

To see the tongue done and bound like this as in billable
columns—one two three four to find it thus eternally arranged.
Four frozen waterfalls of His saying.

Imagine our earth thus pressed

if each holy page contains eternities
is the book shut then:
rejoicing or otherwise?

Ink sewing itself into the rag'd paper, pulped
from what people have worn about
are these imprints a worldly making
of the inbetween subterraneal and heavenly—
type form, tympan—
the captured air words of just above
our heads grabbed down and pressed
to paper—as retrieved
saints to the gravestone,
what limited immortalization
we are capable of with this press
taking language of all God's intermediaries
we have deduced
and designed to our own designs
this bookblock as the
compressed aviary for captured
saints—yet most sense not
the tension in binding these pages.

(Grace liberating all our waste paper and canceled pages to some
looser natural pupose. I see her.)

Like a native tongue (to your mouth)
laid out babbling from God's beginning of time
even running past you to Revelation—such a totality of noise.
And where do we stand?
Between the last page of Jude and the first of Revelation!
We are right now two inches of un-inked paper. Good luck and
God bide you.

Or even just a notation of the noise of our own Godliness that

was going from beginning and will not be gone for it is now inked
out of air which does not add one corpuscle to God's Vast
Existent, anyway. It does make an airspace in translation—then
leaves its absence.
Makes something where there was pure nothing
and leaves then worse than nothing.

Finished: the Book: the Bible: *Up-Biblum God*: in hand,
it is like four soft bricks two by two, a building block, knocked
together. No pocket-book, this. A chunk of truth. Takes two
hands or one with also forearm as one carries the precious babes
a responsibility
some thing.
We do indeed need two praying hands to hold it—such divine
design.

It is bound up but then the binding needs not breaking but
smooth wearing-in as a boot or saddle, walked or ridden, with
your praying hands.

I want to breathe it.

[Robert Boyle: to John Eliot, April 1664]

'I waited this day upon the King with your translation of the Bible.'

[Eliot: of His Children Dying]

One by one they fall, they go, they rise.
I see them like trees.
In their absence
from the field around me,
the field of vision
I labor in, the field I hobble back to
especially each day to see
what is not as once there. The clear space
hardly innominate. Gone. But what was that space
before their passed presences? Any blank space
is God. They were all there in that space. One by one four sons
go, until but Anne and the one boy, the daughter. Gone.
Godspace, their presence in it, their absence from it, Godspace.
The one boy—Joseph, like a holy but half-used father to me, to
the Indians. Oh Anne. Soon she will not return to me, but I will
go unto her. 'My desire was that they should serve God on earth;
but if God will choose rather to have them serve him in heaven, I
have nothing to object against it, his will be done
to take my family to himself' and I
will bear the toothed metal of time
gnashing about me, the work unfinished,
the field wide open and white
but a want of workers.
We must finish.

[Sassamon: of Her]

Grace Indian.
In the tent, now
long hemp dress. Brown and bare, no beads no shoes and the suck
of the flap sliding behind her, pressing shut so we are closed in to
each other. The swish of hardlight is the last word we speak.
Between us the air in the room I've been talking. She will not
move away from the opening. I am sitting at the edge of the mat
looking through the embers. With her hands behind her. I must
get up and move through the words.

My face in her cold hair hides there. Neck, ear, hair hides me
complete. A mask for my face, filter my mouth. Her hair is my
eyes, neck my cheek, ear my mouth. Stay here. Grab her moaning
birdhands and land them on me. Wings folding unfolding and
flapping. Flying the air of my skin. The taste of ocean in her ear,
the soft opening of her hearing wet.

Lift her arms and leave them like exclamation points above us and
bend and pull the brown dress up the stomach and then through
her arms clearing out the air. Dive into her belly where our skin
meets the words press into water wet current of actual contact.
Her cool breath against my sweat I can feel the things evaporate.
The air above us. Smoke. I'm swimming, pushing
soft bird sounds out her mouth
breathing my own air of hers,
shouldering open her shoulders and arms
entering into a good long noise in my head like summer
we loop through mouths
circle, circulate
above at the ears and below
she fully exhales—her expiration condenses my hearing
we both let go
to get

a better grip—birds scatter and re-land
to listen to the liquid
shift of us. A rhythmic report
we waterfall.

Lying there. Kept warm by her dress and a blanket I pulled. I am
stuck to her thigh. And her birds pant on the ground telling this
in twitches.
Something in the outside light flies away, shadow ripping at the
flap.
And the dusk and air off the hill comes under the flap. Sniff it.
Snow, or maybe-snow. She hasn't taken one step further into the
wigwam. Her clean quiet fills it. Draw the whole day across her
like a quilt.

I can't normal noise. And I do not mind it.

Everyone is outside. And the sound of maybe-snow.
I cry a little.
I pray to Christ.

'nummatchekodtantamoonganunnonash'
'our lusts'
'aninnumaiinnean'
'Lord help us'

The next day she gave me her hand—a rare hemming in of her own manual capacities—and into the wood we went. To a young tree she'd stripped of leaves replacing same with the loose marred pages she'd filched from the press floor. Wonder at the sight to see these New Tossed Leaves tied to a tree turning over and over in the breeze a constant rereading of the whole thing each moment.

She pressed to my hand a stitched book leather bound made of that same tree's real leaves. A book of leaves!—how this one listens. Each page imprinted from her finger imbrued in what I take to be her own blood. With occasional other such imprints as lips, breast, fist part, foot part, eyelash (?), &c.

Then she placed me opposite her upon some swept ground there and read from me the entire book. Her mouth actually moving and making sound and sounds. By and by I had the sense of it, but there came no visual translation—it was like constructed white wings unfolding out into more of themselves (though any third observer, any audience, would have heard only ignorantly quite unfamiliar sounds) or more simply it communicated of self-consuming formularies of fire.

Then she kissed the book and pressed it to my breast and possession.
Ran off oceanward.

Thus, I took us married.

Within 2 days the children found the tree. Within a week, the English children. And thus Grace had her trailing brood, her own school of schoolchildren. And John and I had no end of troubles.

I walk

everywhere now. No horses for me, no shallops, packets, canoes
with their push of wind. But my feet on the earth—always one
foot, at least, in contact. I do not run or jump, for motion is a
distraction, and it stirs up the molecules.

I do not swim. It's too much like flying, all thrill and bird-vanity,
and when I die, it's not my body that will fly, so I have changed
my training inward and keep the body anchored to earth to allow
the mind.

The idea is to think. Rather, the idea is to be aware, to think
without words—for they are useless tools to me. To me. The
Word of God is not any actual word, fool, but it is inside you—a
still mass that, yes, if whipped into stormy discourse could be like
to an ocean, but which, if left alone to rest in the essence of its
own awareness, goes still & flat & forever into a wide sea-plain to
walk into (become aware into) until the gold watery wheatlight is
your distances and you fall into it, heavenward, still here, your
concerns narrowed, quiet & solitary as a wounded deer—thus,

I walk, and use the topography to map my progression, my
unmoving, my mind—thoughts arise and fall away—no need to
add any proliferating word—each moment discrete as a flower or
a footstep by the wayside, already past and unelaborated and
onward into more road and earth that flows incessantly and
onward, given to us and solid, sustenance and immortal weight,
making food and a buffer against the wind, firmament, it
remains—keep walking, with each step, it remains—each dusty

step its own and yet the same as the last, the one that propelled
you there, nowhere, the earth is there, mind is there.

Natick: Grace. I teach and preach

Walk.

Cambridge: I work the press

Walk.

Boston: I meet the Elders, report on Philip

Walk.

Mt. Hope: I chip away at poor brave endless Philip

[walk]

who is like words to me, an Indian, he is like me, as I have been,
so I am careful always to feel the earth, and move slow the air out
my mouth—for I can see now, I can see this is killing Philip, I can
see, this new world. We all die, but Philip is rushing to it—his
father rushed to the English, Philip is rushing away—and English
are here, so I must anchor him—if not to Christ, at least to some
small patch of earth (I know he will not, but it is earth the
children run by on now anyway as I sit in his tent trying to coax
him down), he disdains me, the children play, I feel the ground, I
let slow those old words, worrying that he will take the death that
buck in Natick was meant to be.
For to let fly at the English is but to loose and lose yourself and
to shoot your own children. And then they will use Philip as a
type and forerunner to invent their own future, their own nation.

I choose words, then.

I try hard. Only I can do this if it is to be done. Philip chose me
to be the one to try—a sign he is willing, but surely the last sign
he will give them. I am the sign. And so

I walk: Natick, Boston, Mt. Hope, being the sign that's trying to
think without words, to be purely aware. In the beginning was the
Word, but then we made words to make ourselves and this
world—I want to be otherworldly, with the first Word.

But among the many knowledges my new silence has brought is
this: Philip knows one thing I also know: the Lord saves only
individual souls and cares not what's English and what's Indian.
The English do care. And while they speak in acres, Philip (I
know) thinks in generations, and his will not be slaves.
Everybody dies.
I walk.
What? he asks, *Think they we be Jews who suffered not even the mighty
Egyptians, who flew over oceans and a whole world to own one free wilderness,
but we will suffer mere English? By God—if he be my God—and I begin to
see how yes he is and has been our God since the sun, and no trembling English
God, what a pathetic mess these people—by this God it will not come to pass. We
are this God's people, and here he chose us to live.*
I would but have you live here, Philip, my brother, it is what I
seek. These children. Your niece Grace is with child.
*Then cease your seeking, John, and stay with us, and preach for us a way to be the
Lord's army.*
The English will ask the same of their preachers, Philip, and John
Eliot will not do it. But some will. But I will not.

And Grace's school. Her flock of un-told children.

So it goes with their childish wild tongues: *Grace School,* they say.
Then *Grace Cool, Grey School, Gray Skull, Great Skull, Greatskull*—which
they mouth into a password, compressing out the vowels almost

to nothing, just a rocking of the tongue from back to teeth to back with airless outbreath. The 's' just the short necessary slip of a bridge, 't' to 'k.' A safe word in the wood: "Grt'skl." A bird call, a breaking of water and branch.

Motto of my lovely little Grt'skls: *Who Hate Instruction, to Destruction*

Their Lessons She Gives:
Writing in the sand seconds ahead of waves.
100 cut lines of "Pray for Grace" from filched marred pages.
Reciting lines as you ember them out.
Maintaining the LeafTree.
Salt water into eyes to cry unto Christ; a way to inhabituate Saviour-love.

Then Grt'skl discovered an ingenious and troublesome printing device: proper pages pressed upon plucked and susceptible leaves (of such & such tree) then set into a hot sunbeam do fade all the leaf but the letter'd. Using the sun to print leaves and leaves of text.

Thus the children began in earnest to print BibleTrees.

Eliot saw a Godly beauty to the effort & its visual result: the holy Word seeming to grow & flourish flutter out of New England soil. But he could not get such an impression into many of the ministers nor godly laymen nor mothers of Grt'skls cutting proper lessons and chores to hunt shark teeth, dissect squirrel for soul, print BibleTrees.

And these New English are not even comparable unto themselves until they are at issue—then they clamp on admirably like a Vice-Eel, whose jaws through and after death hold to a loving lock. A death the Vice-Eel seems to enjoy for the purpose it proves for its needle teeth. My own John is the most admirable &

gentle soul and see what he accomplishes without even use of anger or vengefulness. Imagine him unleashed. Imagine a mad English mother, a vision of Grace Indian within the bounds of her eyes and children.

And yet the Lord tells us *thou shalt teach them diligently unto thy children, and shalt talk of them when thou sittest in thine house, and when thou walkest by the way, and when thou liest down, and when thou riseth up.* This, Grace knows. And she is her own kind of eel.

And Philip, too.

KING PHILIP

[The Taunton Agreement, between King Philip and Plymouth Colony, Sassamon present—April 1671]

'Whereas my Father, my Brother, and my self, have formally submitted ourselves and our People unto the King's majesty of England, and to the Colony of New Plymouth, by solemn covenant under our hand; but I having of late through my indiscretion, and the naughtiness of my heart, violated and broken this my covenant with my friends, by taking up arms, with evil intent against them, and that groundlessly; I being now deeply sensible of my unfaithfulness and folly, do desire at this time solemnly to renew my covenant with my ancient friends, and my father's friends above mentioned, and do desire that this may testify to the world against me if ever I shall again fail in my faithfulness towards them (that I have now, and at all times found so kind to me) or any other of the English Colonies; and as a real pledge of my true intentions for the future to be faithful and friendly, I do freely engage to resign up into the government of New Plymouth, all my English arms, to be kept by them for their security, so long as they shall see reason. For true performance of my promises, I have hereunto set my hand, together with the rest of my council.

The Mark of *P. Philip.*
    Chief Sachem of Pocanoket.'

[Philip and Sassamon]

Philip:

I was Metacom, then I am King Philip. Have I not converted
already?

The caterpillar the cocoon, the salmon fight up river wanting that
proper death—what then if their flesh was not delicious? What
then do we not eat? A flesh and a blood seem to be for us, but
people are not palatable (though will do). Have I sinned? I know
that our tongues divine the limits of what can become good bread
and tell us by taste. Wine makes the braves kill well and a bit
needlessly. What do I need to be or become?

If we are about changing things, money is the temporary
translation. To become a new thing, it is easier to leave a loose
and variable state than to depart directly from what you really
were. So break yourself open first—become spiritual tender—
then simply spend yourself in the right direction. What is all this
worth to them?

Yes, I must convert or yes I might kill them all, might savage and
heathen. So tell me, Translator, howso shall I change, howso do
you wish to translate me: Metacom, King Philip, Disciple of some
third thing more divine than Indian or English?

Sassamon:

If I give you four shilling and you give one pelt. If water
freezes, is taken up
to the ice house in hay.
        If translated,

a thing passes through
its essential meaning (gathering
what it will),
            if converted,
the thing passes
through you (leaving
essence and you
to your essence). Gather what you might mean but feel what
remains. You need not change but are changed.

Water can translate: Cold—Ice—Warm—Water—Fire—Steam
Fire dies: Water. Eat, Drink, Breathe—Slide, Swim, Hide

            Eating snow water, pissing steam on the coldest day is a
lesson in translations.

Of conversion, consider the waterspout:
                        In a storm day the ocean goes
blackflat and clouds mountain the horizon in a left-right line of
nothing will ever be fine. Deer move away from the shore, dark
silk pulled toward England, a speck of waterdust out there as if a
distant rider kicked her up to a canter, and clouds relinquish their
sigh, their outward inclination to escape current state: Waterspout:
Only all water.
Some parts don't come down.

Philip:

Once, it rained seawater and bluefish on Mt. Hope. Miracle? No
miracle? But nothing either you'd ever wager on seeing, or eating
from. Though eat we did that day.
Now they tell me I've sold away the right to fish out from my own
camp.

109

[Philip: of Sassamon]

Thinks he's fancy Indian. Plate licker, shoe lover, I have seen.
Brown face, white ass. I have three daggers on my person and four
more in the room. He looks and feels to be without blade. Unless
that goddam cross. Unless the old dry blood under his lids. As he
considers, thinks like an English. I say, kid, I can see you think.
And he laughs as if there is something like a knowledge I could
not know. That is when I should have killed him. Right now.
Right just then. I missed. And Grace has taken him.

And the spectacle of this child, playing tavern-chess with a giant
oak tree. With me.

With me he talks of God.
Talks to me as if the sod we two walk is separate and a different
soil than our fathers had. Words for our children, for something
he wants to call our future. This last orphan of an entire tribe. He
says this is like this and this is as that—never just this is: never
simply sell Mt. Hope to Plymouth, build three trading posts in
perpetual treaty, wear shoes, sire from some Boston half-breed,
and call this your own new world of peace and corn and low
smoke mud. Be done. Why does he never give the navigation: do
this to gain everlasting peace on this earth?

There is no final deal with these guns. They come as one people,
then put you under 100 competing contracts. Indict on the word
of one bad Indian. Call you a liar pointing only at their own ink
and paper. Labor to make you so—you'd think a man can't kill a
man and war his people without three years of bickering and
paperwork first. Dull. God, their God, they think to hide their
desires and motivations from Him and themselves. We have
folded fish into these fields since there were people and, give three
years, paper, ink, the English will show the mistake in that.
Sassamon acting as their poet, singing well of many things that

are like but not the thing. Get me the final deal, child. Be my
Trinket-Injun, be my minister and slave. I will never obscure my
purpose or practice, I will use you to pure and readily apparent
ends. You knew my father.

And you, they, they knew my father, they bring me to court.

For killing fair game that flew over some fence and died. When
they buy land they think to buy whatever dies there. [Question:] *If
the arrow does fly from my hands to a hart in my own eyes, how be it the meat is
not mine by law?* [Ans:] *By this ink and paper hidden in a desk in Boston, two
days walk from where you bravely bid the buck to give his life. Come stand to talk
on it like women mealing corn, come stand and talk as winter comes on. Come
stand and talk and talk and talk. And talk.* Turkeys. Eunuchs. Tell me have
you ever seen an English woman ever smile at the sight of her
husband's hands or haunches? They look only to what hands hold,
what the paper says or how much there is. Blocks of
unthawed sod in bonnets. But take one for ransom and how they
turn to Indian ways. How they love to say I never. How they never
run away at night and roll close at any mouse noise. English cease
to be English without other English eyes on them—sometimes
one is forced to extinguish all the others just to silence one hyster-
ical woman. They seem not to stand for reason even when their
own actions lead, one by one, to murder their own children. I have
seen some even seem to call for it and the strange relief in their
eyes—their whole life, I measure, to have known and wanted for
this moment of standing alone, sloshing in the blood of everyone
else. But as a group
their cruelty
of cowards, their cruelty,

Christ was no coward and for sport
they are the oddest tribe on earth. Some of my best braves have
taken to fighting battles up to the point of taking captives and
then walking away—saying there is but two or three cougars in an
English town and after that only screaming cats. We are warriors
they say, not shepherds for cowards. I will shepherd any day, I say,
before I stand another day in Boston court among that clucking. I
will convert before I curtsy. I will do the Lord's work.

[Of Grt'skl a-printing Bibletrees about and toward the seaport,]

a crude broadside appears: "The Holy Word Rent Asunder, or
Decrying the Bible Most Recently Unbound for Pagan Purposes."

[Eliot: Written Report of a Two-Day Dialogue between Praying Indians and King Philip]

SAYETH PHILIP: 'Often have I heard of this great matter of praying unto God, and hitherto I have refused. . . . Old Mr. Eliot himself did come unto me. He was in this town, and did persuade me. But we were then in our sports, wherein I have much delighted, and in that temptation, I confess, I did neglect . . . and lost that opportunity . . . . some serious thoughts of accepting the offer, and turning to God . . . . but I have some great objections . . . . great rocks in my way . . . . too hard for me to get down and swallow . . . . if I pray to God . . . . a deadly fall to me and my posterity . . . . then all my men . . . . easily be trod upon by others . . . . I am drowned and overwhelmed . . . . I will never hinder my people . . . . this bringing all to an equality . . . . will bring all to a confusion . . . . the poor to too much boldness . . . . you speak arrows . . . . but I do not think you hurt me . . . . so much beauty and desirableness . . . . still lie soaking in my heart . . . . the rowlings of my thoughts . . . . the disquiet . . . . turnings and tumblings of my mind . . . . I find nothing . . . . nothing in my mind to oppose against what you say . . . . you have a book . . . . bend my mind. . . . . you read it to me. . . . . . breed in my heart . . . . what is written in it? . . . . there be worse men than we Indians be . . . . give me your ground . . . . gainsay the mountainous weight . . . . have I . . . been dead . . . . followed works of darkness . . . . I am wounded . . . . words that come swimming in love . . . . heart storms of grief . . . . my soul is wounded . . . . My heart is bent within me . . . . neither I nor any of my people know how to do it . . . . I did not intend to open

113

and pour . . . .
. . . .
. . . .
. . . .
. . . .
. . . .
. . . .
. . . .
. . . .
have quite lost myself   . . . .
. . . .
. . . .
. . . .
. . . . what may be further off I know not . . . .
. . . .
. . . . full vessels
are ready to run over . . . .'

[Philip: of Limited Atonement]

Amen. For the sweetness of the Lord is amnesia. Squirrels in the trees, the way fields clear closest the meeting house. The good earth can be asked, can be soiled like the soul—reaping what's sown after what grows is ripped out and burned for compost. Only that sets the human body on the right path to getting slow and fat. The birds of heaven enter not the barn. I speak of fertility, I get done what we need. My women will leave you a slave to use or be. We have materials, all made by the hand of God helping himself. We convert sea shells into more and more money—the job takes only what time passes by. Prayerful guns. Patience. The war of the Lord is just and righteous is the good news brought to us. I am made in His image and imagine a fragment of His intention is not taken up with daily means. These Kings and Fathers, they want the fields murdered and transformed for the bread of their children. No, they want the bread of their children—that the loaves simply appear appears best. The real miracle is disappearing the genesis of the bread. The miracle worker brings bread by mysterious, miraculous means. The end: eating. Salvation enters best through the mouth of starvation. God has always been here with us—unbeknownst because our mouths were partnered to enough earth. We were not starving for God yet, but thankful for his game. We did never sin. The English want civilized Indians to bring to God. So they teach the word 'acre,' this is the entrance to their enclosures.

The English make their bread by dividing labor. One knows nothing. But together they know much and trade such with money. I think this is why they like gathering to worship. This is why they fear Grace's Bibletrees inviting each alone to pray alone away.

[Sassamon: of Grace]

In front of me is the dream. Exactly
as I see it always except.

There is always
a flame
a sucking soaring upward taking of words and body
except
me I am standing here
not soaring. There is a tree.

Grace burning in her Bibletree.

They set flame to every green book she made
and did she climb into this
or was she bound?

She is not contained or hunching down
away but strangely stretched limbs to limbs
with the tree, being done fruit
a strange departure of dust upward
of her growth, a new flesh
inside sent away from this horrid
sensorium soaring up amongst the word—burnt
offering of flesh to be read by Him
this going home sucking in
the whole circle round
an upside-down drain sending her
to God a mouth
emptied out a wind the world's
sound

air rushing round my back
sweeping my face

to her ash'd heat of undoing
of being done

I did this
I have dreamt
mistakenly

this was to be me unworded
upward, only me to so beautifully
be extinguished by eating air and heat

the leaves there, gone, flaked shrinking
color of pure ink turning back
to unmarred meaning
mingled with my Grace

ash alphabet babe shaped now only to upward currents an ideal
communication unto Christ

walking round I see
the belly slit
exposing the babe's formed
sweet face to the smoothing flame:

never a breath—
a simple death that needs no daring
to plunge to God's bosom
and be born
there innocent

whose glory bright whose wondrous might whose power imperial
far surpass whatever is here in realms terrestrial that tongues of
men nor saint's pen cannot the same express and therefore I will
be done with duty lest I further transgress both trees and leaves
their dead at once surrender but fire and air unconstrained are

also their dead to tender since the same translates from mortal states to immortality all that survive and be alive in the blink of mine eye

despite these bodies trying to be trees breathing up to forever

Oh Grace.
My child.
I will get for you.

[Eliot: of Grace]

I am so taken tonight beyond my beliefs of what people be. She was a pure being and, I believe, God's agent. If He means more by this or only to show the Unsaved English by their savage murdering I can not now know—but soon all will out, I fear. The Word of God cannot be unbound by a girl, a tree—these fools make two mistakes, 1] to take the world to their own literal translation, 2] to base such on their own unhappy idea of logic. They will see now what He really means. I fear we shall be too near an audience, all of us. Sassamon and Philip sit now heads pressed on the hill above seaport. Both stripped and blacked in charcoal ripped from Grace's rood. Black English eve below them dropping all last light into those orange blooming Bibletrees each an incandescent turret at some distance seeming to twinkle, to smoketalk with the stars, to translate something ahead of heaven.

[Philip: of Total Depravity & Unconditional Election]

Batten my heart, you English God (for you
As yet but whine, plead, beg, and seek to mend),
That I overthrow them first, then bend
Your force to beat, break, bleach, and make me new:
I, like a conquered tribe given a school,
Do in fact understand you, to no end:
Reason, your messenger to me, I should defend,
But he is captured, tortured into Truth:
Yet dearly I would love you, and love this pain,
But am betrothed to your sweet enemy:
Divorce me, untie, or break that knot again,
Take me into you, undress me, for I
—Unless you enthrall me—will not let you be:
Nor remain chaste, excepting you rape me.

Until the English pay their debt to our land, and to the earth's
good are dead, their souls to English heaven ravished, my mind is
set on heavenly things. If, forced by many treaties, I resign myself
to you, it only buys what has always been mine. I see that you love
the English well, but will not choose me. Your Satan hates me, yet
puts me to loving use. Irresistible grace they say—if I but repent
to their ways—will be mine. Should I

be washed in Christ's blood, which has this ugly might: that being
red, it dyes red souls to white? Or should I ask you to help
unnleash my healthful sins to do as they have done—kill people
where they sleep, and be pressed to hell? Why does intent and
action, born in me, make one life on this earth—mine—more
heinous? And mercy being easy and glorious to you, why threaten
me? Here I am

to treaty with thee: O God, if your red and warlike blood and
their tears make a heavenly cleansing flood, let's ally to drown

them in that sad holy savagery. I will send them all to you, rest for their scalps and souls' delivery. They will wake eternally and fear not you God, finally, for Death is from me.

[Sassamon: Having Warned the English]

Boston.
I walk.
Assawampsett Pond is a solid ice shelf
above air and where water
recedes to—to walk
off earth over
water, over cold sliver of sky,
on such a firm present-tense Revelation
of elements running ahead
and stopped out of time
as my people their country now
is calling the world
as it comes with endless hunger
for our trade and products,
tobacco and furs, so too
will it soon turn trembling
to Godly trundles
and gape
for our spiritual treasures.
Governor Winslow cares not
for my words, my mouth
of warning. I see they (being stuck
in new trade) are as done with me
as I am (seeking Grace everywhere) myself this dawn
watching thoughts wordlessly
arrive, wiggle around, depart
as birds, as seasons,
as English and Indian—I see
God as form, as any, these scenes
in front of me I have burned
into me not thinking words
just the pure vision of what my eyes
do actually appear to, stones,

the moon, what I apprehend
holds in my mind for analysis:
it is always only
dissolution supported by constant
low hum of God, Christ, Ghost, Air,
Earth, Water,
I open my eyes unto them
in all things, and Grace,
the babe
this grey ice
slicing half the seeping-red
sun closes my eyes
on them emerging from
all things
bird cries open
my eyes onto three
dim figures fast approaching
at last.

EPILOGUE

'June 24 (Midsummer-day) At the conclusion of that day of Humiliation, as soon as ever the people of Swansea were come from the place where they had been praying together, the Indians discharged a volley of shot whereby they killed one man and wounded others. Two men were sent to call a Surgeon for the relief of the wounded, but the Indians killed them by the way: and in another part of the town six men were killed, so that there were nine English men murthered this day.

'Thus did the War begin, this being the first English blood which was spilt by the Indians in a hostile way.'

[Eliot: 'To the right honorable Robert Boyle, Esq., Governor of the Corporation for the Gospelizing the Indians,' 1675]

'I must change my ditty now.

'The work (in our patent) is under great sufferings. It is killed in words, wishes, and expression, but not in deeds. As yet it is (as it were) dead but not buried; nor (I believe) shall be. It is made conformable to Christ (in some poor measure) in dying, but I believe it shall rise again.

'There be three hundred and fifty souls or thereabout put upon a bleak, bare island, the fittest we have, where they suffer hunger and cold; there is neither food nor competent fuel to be had, and they are bare in clothing, because they cannot be received to work for clothing, as they were wont to do. Our rulers are careful to order them food, but it is so hard to be performed that they suffer much. I beg your prayers that the Lord would take care of them and provide for them. I cannot without difficulty, hardship, and peril get unto them.'

[Eliot: to the Society for the Propagation of the Gospel in New England]

Sirs,
The sermon of the day is: physicians,
books, the lost tribe of knowledge
is forecast to unmanifest
its fatal arrows: we operate
in this drastic forest of articulate sounds,
please send bread and fish: starving guttural
sounds aspirate at back the throat, where we
shy from letting our own thoughts go
even so deep: the way we think 'Devil'
where 'Oak' and 'Fir' cloak their universal
sense and church, their not having words
and we have nothing to carry them
outside our own tongues: *For he that speaketh*
in an unknown tongue speaketh not unto man,
but unto God: Sirs, four hundred red souls
starve on Deer Isle, selecting stones,
as other sermons run to prophecies
and fort defense:
daily we drown in discovering
loose heads strewn on the highway
as in the Bible: we must translate this
universal nourishment to *all* their tongues:
every instrument set to work
does press for pay, and in this desert
the sermon of the day prays
the biggest boats closer, waves
the marked arm rising off Death Isle, says bring
budgets and bring butter and that best Word:
the least generous omniscience of our own
utter limit unto death (or coming into sight)
of those yet tasting what charity and what,

already, we are capable of having done. *What?*
came the word of God out from you? or did it come
to you *only?* The press needs also
twelve pounds each of fresh 'k's and 'l's to conform
this ancient Hebraic language
to the rules of our alphabet. We,
meaning English, burn the Bible
quick as we can print it
in this tribe's lost tongue
we are losing.

[Eliot: To the Honorable, the Governor & Council at Boston, 1675]

'The humble petition of John Eliot

'Sheweth
'That the terror of selling away such Indians, unto the islands for perpetual slaves, who shall yield up themselves to your mercy, is like to be an effectual prolongation of the war and such an exasperation of them, as may produce we know not what evil consequences upon all the land. Christ hath said, *blessed are the merciful, for they shall obtain mercy.* This usage of them is worse than death. To put to death men that have deserved to die is an ordinance of God, & a blessing is promised to it. It may be done in Faith. The design of Christ in these last days is not to extirpate nations, but to gospelize them. When we came, we declared to the world, and it is recorded, yes we are engaged by our letter Patent to the King's Majesty, that the endeavor of the Indians' conversion, not their extirpation, was one great end of our enterprise in coming to these ends of the earth. It seemeth to me, that to sell them away for slaves is to hinder the enlargement of his kingdom. How can a Christian soul yield to act, in casting away their souls for whom Christ hath with an eminent hand provided an offer of the gospel—to sell souls for money seemeth to me a dangerous merchandise.
'If they deserve to die, it is far better to be put to death, under godly governors, who will take religious care that means may be used that they die penitently. To sell them away from all means of grace, when Christ hath provided means of grace for them, is the way for us to be active in the destroying their souls, when we are highly obliged to seek their conversion, & salvation, & have opportunity in our hands so to do. The Country is large enough, here is land enough for them & us too.'

[Philip Shot Dead in the Great Swamp, August 12, 1676]

And 'Capt. Church ordered his body to be pull'd out of the mire on
      the Upland,
so some of Capt. Church's Indians took hold of him by his
      Stockings,

and some by his small Breeches, (being otherwise naked) and drew
      him thro' the mud
unto the upland, and a doleful, great, naked, dirty beast, he look'd
      like.

Capt. Church then said, *That forasmuch as he had caused many an English
      man's body*
to lie unburied and rot above ground, that not one of his bones should be buried.

And calling his old Indian Executioner, bid him behead and quarter
      him.
Accordingly, he came with his hatchet and stood over him,

but before he struck he made a small speech directing it to Philip;
and said, *He had been a very great Man, and had made many a man afraid of him,*

but so big as he was, he would now chop his Ass for him; and so went to work,
and did as he was ordered. Philip having one very remarkable hand

being much scarr'd, occasioned by the splitting of a pistol in it
      formerly,
Capt. Church gave the head and that hand to Alderman, the Indian
      who shot him,

to show such Gentlemen as would bestow gratuities upon him;
and accordingly he got many a penny by it.'

Afterword:
The Poetry, The Invention

THE POETRY

Language—in every moment of history making—creates its own structures of meaning and carries them forward.

This book of poetry enters a set of events (through their limited archival records) whose moments of history-making are tangled and deep, and unwinds them by sounding out the currents of those events' extant language (as well as the currents of a few other universal habits of the human animal). This poetry is not working to pursue the facts of the archive, which are anything but objective, but to confound them back into the full color and subjectivity of lived experience.

There are facts. And then there are words—our tools for trying to move facts forward, whether with integrity or deceit. Facts are fine things, they are the starting points we claim, and we often imagine we use them in our lives, but they are rarely the actual means or ends for people. We are in flux, and we use words to navigate. To wit, the events—things done by people—this book passes through:

The translated Bible, the languages, the words.
The converted souls.
The land grab.
The human affections, the human violence.
The spiritual conviction.
The project of colonialism.
The project of survival.

Words, souls, blood, land, language—in translation.

In this mix there was, and is, scant solid resting place for fact. Everything is in a state of communication, of derangement and rearrangement, of remembering and forgetting. The best thing this book can hope to do is to enter the language and human habits of these moments, acclimate to their rhythms and logics, and then run with those toward truths that lie beyond the scope of the so-called historical record. What those truths might be, readers may begin to sense.

All source material used here is from the 17th century and appears in single quotes. As the slimmest possible membrane between archival "facts" and the momentum of the languages and experiences constrained in those incomplete texts—the momentum that plays out this book—these single quotes may be forgotten, ignored, or missed by readers. The only thing they tell you, anyhow, is where the archival records stops caring about the lives of these characters. The extant 17th-century records of these events, we should keep in mind, were all written or controlled by the English.

Those readers interested in pursuing the archival sources and their gaps, competing historical facts, and varying interpretations should begin with the bibliography.

THE INVENTION

The character of Grace Indian does not appear in the historical record, nor does any record of direct correspondence between John Sassamon and Robert Bolye. Eliot's wife, Anne, is all but invisible in the historical record. Sassamon was only one among many natives who worked with the English, whether as linguists, church teachers in Indian towns, or printers. A Nipmuc known as James Printer, who also attended classes as Harvard, worked extensively with the press in Cambridge and likely did the bulk of the printing work for the translated Bible. All of the political events in this book of poetry are events in the historical record, such as it is. All of the human interactions are, by necessity and inevitablity, imagined.

HISTORICAL TIMELINE

[adapted from Kawashima and Lepore]

c. 1620 John Sassamon born

1631 John Eliot immigrates to Massachusetts Bay

1632 Eliot starts missionary work among the Indians and meets Sassamon

1637 Sassamon serves English in Pequot War

1646 Eliot begins preaching in the Massachusett language

1647 Eliot begins publishing promotional tracts in England

1650 Praying Town of Natick established

1651 Sassamon appointed schoolmaster in Eliot's praying town of Natick

1653-4 Sassamon attends Harvard

1654 Eliot publishes his first book in Massachusett

1661 Philip's father Massasoit dies. Philip's brother Wamsutta (Alexander) becomes chief sachem of the Wampanoags. Sassamon becomes his official secretary

1662 Alexander dies. Philip becomes chief Sachem, with Sassamon as his secretary

1663 First edition of the complete Massachusett Bible is printed in Cambridge, Massachusetts

c. 1669 Sassamon returns to Natick

1671 Philip forced to sign a new treaty with Plymouth Colony (The Taunton Agreement). Eliot sends Sassamon to attempt to convert Philip

1673 Sassamon deeded land in Namasket, where he becomes minister

1674 Sassamon meets with Philip

1675 January: Sassamon travels to Plymouth to warn English of Philip's military plans
January 29: Sassamon found dead in Assawampsett Pond

1675 March: Philip's men Tobias, Wampapaquan, and Mattashunannamo are indicted for Sassamon's murder
June 8: Tobias and Mattashunannamo are executed

June 19: Wampanoags attack Swansea; war begins
1676   August 12: Philip killed

BIBLIOGRAPHY

Seventeenth-Century Material

Note: While the title pages for many of the linguistic and spiritual works below often credit only John Eliot as the author or translator, he did this work in collaboration with uncredited native translators.

Letters of John Eliot

- *Jews in America*, or *Probablilites, that those Indians are Judaical,* Thomas Thorowgood, 1660 (includes a letter from Eliot to Thorowgood).
- *John Eliot and the Indians, 1652-1657; being letters addressed to Rev. Jonathan Hanmer of Barnstable, England, reproduced from the original manuscripts in the possession of Theodore N. Vail.* 1915.
- A letter of the Reverend John Eliot of Roxbury to the Reverend Thomas Shepard of Charlestown, August 22, 1673 concerning the state of the gospel work among the Indians.
- Letters by John Eliot to the treasurer and to the governor of the society in London for propagating the gospel among the Indians in America.
- *Memoirs of the life and character of Rev. John Eliot, apostle of the N. A. Indians* by Martin Moore (includes twenty pages of letters from Eliot to Hon. Robert Boyle).
- Petition of the Rev. John Eliot, August 1675. (in *Records of the Colony of New Plymouth*).
- *The New England Company of 1649 and John Eliot: The Ledger for the Years 1650-1660 and the Record Book of Meetings Between 1656 and 1668 of the Corporation for the Propagation of the Gospel in New England.* 1.
- *Some Correspondence Between the Governors and Treasurers of the New England Company in London and the Commissioners of the United Colonies in America, the Missionaries of the Company and Others Between the Years of 1657 and 1712.* 1896.

- *Some unpublished correspondence of the Reverend Richard Baxter and the Reverend John Eliot.* 1931.
- *Three letters of John Eliot and a bill of lading of the Mayflower.* 1919.

Linquistic Works

- *The Indian Grammar Begun: Or, An Essay to bring the Indian Language into Rules, For the Help of such as desire to Learn the same, for the furtherance of the Gospel Among them,* by John Eliot. 1666.
- *The Indian primer; or, The way of training up of our Indian youth in the good knowledge of God,* by John Eliot. 1669.
- *The Logick Primer,* by John Eliot. 1672.
- *New England's Prospect,* by William Wood. 1634.

Spiritual Works

- *Bible.* Algonquian. [*Mamusse Wunneetupanatamwe Up-Biblum God*] Eliot. 1663.
- *Bible.* O.T. Genesis. Algonquian. Eliot. 1655. (The first nineteen chapters have English words interlined with the Algonquian text.)
- *A brief answer to a small book written by John Norcot against infant-baptisme,* by John Eliot. 1678.
- *Christiane oonoowae sampoowaonk = A Christian covenanting confession,* by John Eliot. 1660.
- *Communion of churches,* by John Eliot. 1665.
- *The Dying speeches of several Indians,* translated by John Eliot. 1685.
- *The Massachusett psalter or, Psalms of David with the Gospel according to John, in columns of Indian and English.: Being an introduction for training up the aboriginal natives, in reading and understanding the Holy Scriptures,* by Experience Mayhew. (This psalter gives English lines to match lines from the Algonquian Bible.) 1709.
- *May, waj who nashpe nutayi mun wahshae wunauchemookae moeuweekomunk, ut oowesuonganis Jesus Chris. = The way we walk in when we call up the Indian towns*

and parishes into the order of visible Gospel churches, by John Eliot. 1658.
- *The New Testament of our Lord and Saviour Jesus Christ. Translated into the Indian Language.* John Eliot. 1661.

The "Eliot Tracts"

- *A Brief Narrative of the Progress of the Gospel amongst the Indians in New England, in the Year 1670.* 1671.
- *The Clear Sun-shine of the Gospel breaking forth upon the Indians in New-England.* 1648.
- *The Day-Breaking, if not the Sun-Rising of the Gospell with the Indians in New-England.* 1647.
- *A further Accompt of the Progresse of the Gospel amongst the Indians in New England With Some Helps for the Indians by Abraham Pierson.* 1659.
- *A further Account of the progress of the Gospel amongst the Indians in New England.* 1660.
- *The Glorious Progress of the Gospel amongst the Indians of New England.* 1649.
- *A Late and Further Manifestation of the Progress of the Gospel amongst the Indians in New England.* 1655.
- *The Light appearing more and more towards the perfect Day or a farther discovery of the present state of the Indians in New England.* 1651.
- *New Englands First Fruits.* 1643.
- *Strength out of Weaknesse, Or a Glorious Manifestation of the Further Progresse of the Gospel among the Indians in New England.* 1652.
- *Tears of Repentance: Or, A further Narrative of the Progress of the Gospel amongst the Indians in New-England.* 1653.

Scientific Works

- *An Essay Of the Great Effects Of Even Languid and Unheeded Motion. Whereunto is Annexed An Experimental Discourse of some little observed Causes of the Insalubrity and Salubrity of the Air and its Effects,* by Robert Boyle. 1685.

- *The General History of the Air Designed and Begun by the Honble. Robert Boyle Esq.*, Robert Boyle. 1692.

Puritan War Reporting

- *A Relacion of the Indyan Warre*, John Easton, 1675.
- *The Present State of New-England with Respect to the Indian War*, N.S., 1675.
- *A Continuation of the State of New-England*, N.S., 1676.
- *A New and Further Narrative of the State of New-England*, N.S., 1676.
- *A Brief History of the Warr with the Indians in New-England*, Increase Mather, 1676.
- *An Earnest Exhortation To the Inhabitants of New-England*, Increase Mather, 1676.
- *The Warr in New-England Visibly Ended*, by R.H., 1677.
- *A Narrative of the Troubles with the Indians of New England*, William Hubbard, 1677.

Further Reading in Secondary Sources

- *The Common Pot: The Recovery of Native Space in the Northeast.* Lisa Brooks, 2008.
- *Dry Bones and Indian Sermons: Praying Indians in Colonial America.* Kristina Bross, 2004.
- *Early Native Literacies in New England: A Documentary and Critical Anthology.* Kristina Bross and Hilary E. Wyss, editors, 2008.
- *Igniting King Philip's War: The John Sassamon Murder Trial.* Yasuhide Kawashima, 2001.
- *The Invasion of America: Indians, Colonialism, and the Cant of Conquest.* Francis Jennings, 1975.
- *Indian Deeds: The Land Transactions of Plymouth Colony, 1620-1691.* Jeremy Dupertuis Bangs, 2002.
- *John Eliot's First Indian Teacher and Interpreter, Cockenoe-De-Long Island, And the Story of His Career From the Early Records.* William Wallace Tooker, 1896.

- *John Eliot's Mission to the Indians before King Philip's War.* Richard W. Cogley, 1999.
- *Manitou and Providence: Indians, Europeans, and the Making of New England, 1500-1643.* Neal Salisbury, 1982.
- *New England Frontier: Puritans and Indians, 1620-1675.* Alden T. Vaughn, 1995.
- *So Dreadfull a Judgement: Puritan Repsonses to King Philip's War 1676-1677.* Richard Slotkin and James K. Folsom, editors, 1978.
- *The Name of War: King Philip's War and the Origins of American Identity.* Jill Lepore, 1999.
- *The Puritan Conversion Narrative: The Beginnings of American Expression.* Patricia Cladwell, 1983.
- *Writing Indians: Literacy, Christianity, and Native Communities in Early America.* Hilary E. Wyss, 2000.

The Author

Robert Strong is the founding editor of Poetic Research at *Common-place* and has received fellowships from the Massachusetts Historical Society and the American Antiquarian Society. Previous books include *Puritan Spectacle, Joyful Noise: An Anthology,* the chapbook *Brethren: Order of the Seasons,* and the conceptual fiction *Manufact Hologram.* He teaches at Bates College in Maine.

THE MARIE ALEXANDER POETRY SERIES

Founded in 1996 by Robert Alexander, the Marie Alexander Poetry Series is dedicated to promoting the appreciation, enjoyment, and understanding of American prose poetry. Currently an imprint of White Pine Press, the series publishes one to two books annually. These are typically single-author collections of short prose pieces, sometimes interwoven with lineated sections, and an occasional anthology demonstrating the historical or international context within which American poetry exists. It is our mission to publish the very best contemporary prose poetry and to carry the rich tradition of this hybrid form on into the 21st century.

Series Editor: Robert Alexander
Editor: Nickole Brown

Volume 21
Bright Advent
Robert Strong

Volume 20
Nothing to Declare: A Guide to the Flash Sequence
Edited by Robert Alexander, Eric Braun & Debra Marquart

Volume 19
To Some Women I Have Known
Re'Lynn Hansen

Volume 18
The Rusted City
Rochelle Hurt

Volume 17
Postage Due
Julie Marie Wade